Embracing God's Plan for Marriage

A Bible Study for Couples

W9-CCA-270

Mark and Melanie Hart

Rec. 7/24/22

Embracing God's Plan for Marriage

A Bible Study for Couples

Mark and Melanie Hart

theWORD
among us®
press

Copyright © 2012 by Mark and Melanie Hart
All rights reserved

The Word Among Us Press
7115 Guilford Road
Frederick, Maryland 21704
www.wau.org
16 15 14 13 12   1 2 3 4 5

ISBN: 978-1-59325-204-5

Nihil Obstat: The Rev. Michael Morgan, Chancellor
Censor Librorum
April 9, 2012
Imprimatur: + Most Rev. Felipe J. Estévez, STD, Bishop of St. Augustine
April 9, 2012

Scripture texts used in this work are taken from the New Revised Standard Version Bible: Catholic Edition, copyright © 1989. 1993, Division of Christian Education of the National Council of the Churches of Christ in the USA. All rights reserved. Used with permission.

Excerpts from the English translation of the *Catechism of the Catholic Church* for use in the United States of America, copyright © 1994, United States Catholic Conference, Inc.—Libreria Editrice Vaticana. Used with permission.

Cover and text design by David Crosson
Photo by Carlos Weaver

No part of this publication may be reproduced, stored in a retrieval system, or transmitted in any form or by any means—electronic, mechanical, photocopy, recording, or any other—except for brief quotations in printed reviews, without the prior permission of the author and publisher.

Made and printed in the United States of America

Library of Congress Cataloging-in-Publication Data

Hart, Mark, 1973-
Embracing God's plan for marriage : a Bible study for couples / Mark and Melanie Hart.
p. cm.
ISBN 978-1-59325-204-5
1. Marriage—Biblical teaching—Textbooks. I. Hart, Melanie. II. Title.
BS680.M35H37 2012
248.8'44--dc23
2012001795

Contents

Welcome to The Word Among Us Keys to the Bible   6

Introduction: 9
     Scripture: The Instruction Manual for Marriage

Session 1: The Two Becoming One   12
     Embracing the Divine Design

Session 2: Filling the Void   30
     It Takes Three to Be Married

Session 3: Tearing Down False Temples   44
     When the Soul Leads the Body

Session 4: On a Mission from God   60
     Dying to Ourselves

Session 5: Your Home as the Domestic Church   76
     Unleashing the Virtues

Session 6: The Weekly Wedding Feast   90
     An Invitation to Intimacy

Practical Pointers for Your Bible Study Sessions   107

Sources and Acknowledgments   110

Welcome to
The Word Among Us
Keys to the Bible

Have you ever lost your keys? Everyone seems to have at least one "lost keys" story to tell. Maybe you had to break a window of your house or wait for the auto club to let you into your car. Whatever you had to do probably cost you—in time, energy, money, or all three. Keys are definitely important items to have on hand!

The guides in The Word Among Us Keys to the Bible series are meant to provide you with a handy set of keys that can "unlock" the treasures of the Scriptures for you. Scripture is God's living word. Within its pages we meet the Lord. So as we study and meditate on Scripture and unlock its many treasures, we discover the riches it contains—and in the process, we grow in intimacy with God.

Since 1982, *The Word Among Us* magazine has helped Catholics develop a deeper relationship with the Lord through daily meditations that bring the Scriptures to life. More than ever, Catholics today desire to read and pray with the Scriptures, and many have begun to form small faith-sharing groups to explore the Bible together.

We designed the Keys to the Bible series after conducting a survey among our magazine readers to learn what they wanted in a Catholic Bible study. We found that they were looking for easy-to-understand, faith-filled materials that approach Scripture from a clearly Catholic perspective. Moreover, they wanted a Bible study that would show them how they could apply what they learn from Scripture to their everyday lives. They also asked for sessions that they could complete in an hour or two.

Our goal was to design a simple, easy-to-use Bible study guide that would also be challenging and thought provoking. We hope that this guide fulfills those admittedly ambitious goals. We are confident, however, that taking the time to go through this guide—whether by yourself, with a friend, or in a small group—will be a worthwhile endeavor that will bear fruit in your life.

How to Use the Guides in This Series

The study guides in the Keys to the Bible series are divided into six sessions that each deal with a particular aspect of the topic. Before starting the first session, take the time to read the introduction, which sets the stage for the sessions that follows. Be sure to begin each session with prayer. Ask God to open his word to you and speak to you in a personal way. Read each Scripture passage slowly and carefully. Then, take as much time as you need to meditate on the passage and pursue any thoughts it brings to mind. When you are ready, move on to the accompanying commentary, which offers various insights into the text.

Two sets of questions are included in each session to help you "mine" the Scripture passage and discover its relevance to your life. Those under the heading "Understand!" focus on the text itself and help you grasp what it means. Occasionally a question allows for a variety of answers and is meant to help you explore the passage from several angles within your vocation. "Grow!" questions are intended to elicit a personal response from you by helping you examine your life in light of the values and truths that you uncover through your study of the Scripture passage and its setting. Under the headings "Reflect!" and "Act!" we offer suggestions to help you respond concretely to the challenges posed by the passage.

Finally, pertinent quotations from the Fathers of the Church as well as insights from contemporary writers appear throughout each session. Coupled with relevant selections from the *Catechism of the Catholic Church* and information about the history, geography, and culture of first-century Palestine, these selections (called "In the Spotlight") add new layers of understanding and insight to your study.

As is true with any learning resource, you will benefit the most from this study by writing your answers to the questions in the spaces provided. The simple act of writing can help you formulate your thoughts more clearly—and will also give you a record of your reflections and spiritual growth that you can return to in the future to see how much God has accomplished in your life. End your reading or study with a prayer thanking God for what you have learned—and ask the Holy Spirit to guide you in living out the call you have been given as a Christian in the world today.

Although the Scripture passages to be studied and the related verses for your reflection are printed in full in each guide (from the New Revised Standard Version: Catholic Edition), you will find it helpful to have a Bible on hand for looking up other passages and cross-references or for comparing different translations.

The format of the guides in The Word Among Us Keys to the Bible series is especially well suited for use in small groups. Since this particular study is designed for couples, we recommend that you use it together, as a couple, rather than in a small group. Reading the guidelines on pages 107–109 before you begin will help you get the most out of this study.

We pray that this guide will not only bless your marriage but that it will also unleash the fullness of the grace and power of your sacrament. As blessed as your marriage currently may be, there are assuredly even more graces awaiting you when you humbly ask God to grow in holiness through the Sacrament of Marriage and in your love for one another.

The Word Among Us Press

Introduction

Scripture: The Instruction Manual for Marriage

How does one judge a successful marriage? By how long the marriage lasts? That might be one clue, but plenty of people stay in unhappy marriages without getting separated and divorced, and some great marriages are cut short by early death, or they begin later in life.

So what does a good marriage look like? Since God created marriage, he must have a plan for it in mind, and that plan cannot be based on our failings but on his perfection. He is always going to expect more from us and desire more for us, because allowing us to settle for anything less than perfection (which is God) would not be authentic love. Indeed, "we love because he first loved us" (1 John 4:19).

We do have an instruction manual for a successful, happy, and holy marriage: the written word of God. Sacred Scripture is a lighthouse, guiding us back to God and his family, especially when we are being tossed about on the seas of pride, sinfulness, suffering, and discontent. Scripture is a herald, constantly leading us forward toward Christ and further along than we ourselves think (or feel) we can go.

The Bible is very specific; everything we need—every truth necessary for a healthy marriage—is available to us, if only we have the eyes to read, the ears to hear, and the heart to receive. Most people miss out on all that marriage has to offer, the gift that God intended it to be. God wants our marriages to bless us and fulfill us on innumerable levels. For both husband and wife, marriage is a path to self-discovery and sanctity.

The Great Gift of Sacramental Marriage

This Bible study can help couples embrace God's plan for marriage. When we have little to no idea of what that plan is, however, we can't tap into the grace of the sacrament or unleash the Holy Spirit's power to help and guide us. Sacramental marriage is one of the greatest gifts ever bequeathed to humankind. Understanding what true love entails and offers, what inhibits it, and how grace works to overcome our weaknesses is the key to not only a "successful" marriage but to a holy, happy, and passionate one. God is waiting to fill all the gaps of our humanity with the experience of his divinity.

Sometimes our own thinking can act as an obstacle to a loving, fulfilling marriage. We may simply be afraid of embracing or seeking it. We may say, "It's too late." We may claim that our spouse will never change—or deep down, we may be unwilling to change ourselves. We may view a truly intimate, sacrificial marriage as a pure fairy tale that is utterly unattainable; when we look around to our extended families and parishes, we may wonder if anyone is truly capable of it. We may even take on a very reactionary posture. We might say to our spouses, "You put me first *first*, and then I'll do the same." We assume that love means to give . . . *and to take.*

But there is no "take" in the crucifix. Jesus, hands nailed to the cross, *took* nothing. It's in the shadow of the cross that we are reminded of true sacrifice—that's one reason why the Church requires that Catholic weddings take place in a church at the altar. Love doesn't know how to take. Love only gives. Yet we often want to hold on to the right to withhold or even revoke our love if our spouses do not reciprocate.

Make no mistake: In marriage, as in any other vocation to which God has called us, we must die to ourselves in order to live in Christ (2 Corinthians 5:15; Galatians 2:20). That's where the *mystery* comes in, and that mystery is divine. This is a mystery to behold, not to be "solved." There are many Catholics who don't have this type of marriage; there are many who have given up hope. The sacrament, however, is stronger than we are; God's grace is always stronger than our sin. Vocations are supposed to unearth in us a better version of ourselves. We should not lie in wait, wondering whether or not a marriage is or is not fulfilling its potential, goal, or purpose. Because it is a sacrament, our vocation to marriage is designed to unleash the Holy Spirit's power in our lives. To settle for less is to settle for the earthly while the heavenly beckons us to far greater.

In the six sessions that follow, we are going to peer into the very heart of God, offering open hearts and fresh eyes to ancient truths. Some of the passages you might know well, and others you might be encountering for the very first time. The truths God breathed into these sacred texts are both comforting and afflicting to modern hearts and, assuredly, to modern marriages. You might find yourself challenged at times, but *do not* feel hopeless. If your marriage—or the marriages of those you love—is not currently "measuring up" to God's design, trust that it can improve *daily* with his help and grace.

There's no time like the present to invite the Holy Spirit into your relationship in a new way. There's no reason your sacrament can't be healed or grow even stronger in the days to come. It all begins with a prayer—an invitation to allow God to have his way in your heart, your home, and your relationship.

Before a husband and wife can truly "become one," each has to be one with God. So before you turn this page, say a prayer. God, the author of your life and of your marriage, has something he wants to say to you, right now.

Mark and Melanie Hart

Embracing the Divine Design

Genesis 1:26-28

[26]Then God said, "Let us make humankind in our image, according to our likeness; and let them have dominion over the fish of the sea, and over the birds of the air, and over the cattle, and over all the wild animals of the earth, and over every creeping thing that creeps upon the earth."

[27]So God created humankind in his image,
   in the image of God he created them;
   male and female he created them.

[28]God blessed them, and God said to them, "Be fruitful and multiply, and fill the earth and subdue it; and have dominion over the fish of the sea and over the birds of the air and over every living thing that moves upon the earth."

> Life teaches us, in effect, that love—married love—is the foundation stone of all life.
> —Blessed John Paul II

Genesis 2:21-25

[21]So the LORD God caused a deep sleep to fall upon the man, and he slept; then he took one of his ribs and closed up its place with flesh. [22]And the rib that the LORD God had taken from the man he made into a woman and brought her to the man. [23]Then the man said,

   "This at last is bone of my bones
      and flesh of my flesh;
   this one shall be called Woman,
      for out of Man this one was taken."

[24]Therefore a man leaves his father and his mother and clings to his wife, and they become one flesh. [25]And the man and his wife were both naked, and were not ashamed.

T he modern mind often struggles with the early chapters of Genesis. In a scientifically savvy, technologically advanced culture such as ours, the creation stories in Genesis 1–2 seem to resemble more of a bedtime fairy tale or mythic folklore than an actual description of how the world came into existence.

However, the Catholic Church does not teach that we must interpret the creation accounts of Genesis scientifically; instead, it teaches us that these chapters contain basic, fundamental truths "revealed by God for our salvation" (*Catechism of the Catholic Church*, 337). The authors of Genesis were concerned not with giving the reader a definitive scientific explanation of "how" the world was created as much as the "why" of creation—of life, of our differences as men and women, of marriage, of sexuality and children. That is the mystery Genesis is inviting us to ponder and enter into.

It's important to note that the selected passages are taken from the two complementary creation accounts given to us in Genesis 1 and 2. Taken together, these accounts teach us different facets of the same creative truth; they are like two expressive sides of the same beautiful coin. The first account exalts man as the pinnacle of God's creative process, ending with the intriguing and vast revelation of our creation in God's very image. The second recounts man coming from dust and woman from a rib. In Genesis 1, God is more mysterious, demonstrating his power and sovereignty from a distance. In the second account, God comes near; he walks with Adam (3:8) and brings life through physical contact (2:21). Here, God is far from distant or mysterious; he is intimate and intentional. In both, God reveals something about himself and his creation. God is both mysterious and accessible, sovereign yet intimate. God is also intentional about all that he creates and the order and purpose for which he creates it.

In the verses that precede the first passage (Genesis 1:1-25), we see both the separation of light from darkness and land from sea, as well as the creation of live creatures such as birds, fish, and animals. But God had bigger plans. No aspect of creation thus far—not even the sunset—had echoed God's radiance like his final creation would. The centerpiece of the Garden of Eden was to be the masterpiece of creation—one made in his own divine image and likeness (1:26). That means that humankind resembles God in certain respects (CCC, 355–368). Although God is infinitely greater and more powerful, Adam and Eve had certain similarities, including the two most important ones: *intellect* and *will*.

God created Adam with an intellect to know truth and to understand and contemplate the things he saw and encountered. He also gave Adam and Eve wills with which to *love*. This is also quite remarkable. God didn't want Adam to be an emotionless logician with no feeling or affections. He also didn't want Adam to be ruled only by physical desires. God wanted humans both to know the truth *and* to love the good—each other and, ultimately, God himself, who is the greatest good.

> God is intentional about all that he creates and the order and purpose for which he creates it.

These gifts of intellect and will are very special. Cats and dogs exist, but they can't know and love God. Birds and fish have life, but not a life in which they can actively worship God. Only man "is called to share, by knowledge and love, in God's own life" (CCC, 356).

Here are other fundamental truths about men and women that can be gleaned from these verses of Genesis:

- God puts Adam to sleep and removes his rib, which is worthy of mention. The woman is being created from the man (Genesis 2:23; 1 Corinthians 11:8-9), and her physical distinction is complementary to his own. This point cannot be glossed over or lost: In God's divine design, the man and woman *are made for each other*. There is a difference, and that difference is *good* (Genesis 1:31). The fact that it was his rib, not his head or heel, speaks to her equality; woman is neither above nor below the man in her dignity (CCC 369–371). Their unique vocations, as man and woman, are intimately tied and inseparable from their unique but equal genders; they are complementary but distinct, as we will unpack further in chapter two.

■ It is God who creates the marriage covenant (Genesis 2:22) and who calls the man and woman to sexual intimacy (2:23-24) that will result in procreation and life (1:28), if God so wills it. Again, God is the impetus and the catalyst for life and the marriage that precedes it.

■ God brings the woman to the man. The woman is being entrusted to the man's protection and care, as his directive was to "keep," or more to the Hebrew author's point, to "guard" the garden and all life within it (Genesis 2:15).

■ Adam and Eve's original state of nakedness points to a selfless innocence, one free of shame (Genesis 2:25). The desire for sex is there, and before the fall, it is pure. However, with sin comes concupiscence (lust), and sexuality becomes skewed. When we abandon God and his plan for our lives, we lose sight of marriage's purpose—we have replaced purpose (what we bring to it) with use (what we take from it). This is when sexuality becomes disordered, when the self-gift of sex is lost and the purpose and the mystery are abandoned for personal and selfish gratification. When we try to separate God the Creator from the creative mystery, we lose the *purpose* and are left merely with *use*.

■ Not only does marriage have a purpose in God's eyes, but man and woman have different purposes, even though they enjoy equal dignity. Their bodies point us back to God's intended design. Woman is more complex biologically than man, and enjoys a unique role within creation as a mother, privileged to participate very uniquely in the act of creation with God, the creator of all human life. We see the roles of men and women woven into the very fabric of their genetic makeup.

■ "Be fruitful" (Genesis 1:28) is a command, but not in a self-serving way, since it cannot (and should not) be separated from the rest of the command, "and multiply" (or the intentionality of multiplying). When the Church, during the wedding vows, asks, "Will you accept children willingly?" there is an understood implication of openness to life on behalf of the couple.

These verses from Genesis offer us a timeless yet somewhat countercultural viewpoint on life and love, marriage and family. Other books on marriage tell us *how* to love; the Bible tells us *why* we love (1 John 4:19). Why did God choose to reveal himself and his plan to us in this way? Why did he create us male and female? Why are those differences important? Genesis helps us to answer those questions—and what they mean for our lives. *Excellent!*

Understand!

1. Why is the ability to love (free will) such a vital complement to our intellect? What would the result be with one or the other but not both?

_____

_____

_____

_____

_____

_____

2. Why would God command humankind be to "be fruitful and multiply" (Genesis 1:28)? What does that tell us about the mind and heart of God? What does this command teach us about how we reflect and experience God's love?

_____

_____

_____

_____

_____

3. In your own words, what is God's intention for marriage? How does it reflect the love between the Father, Son, and Holy Spirit? How does this truth change the way you view your own marriage?

_____

_____

_____

_____

_____

4. How does God's physiological design of the man and woman complement his institution of the marriage covenant? What truths does our physical creation necessarily imply about human sexuality and how it pertains to God's intention for marriage? What does it say about same-sex partnerships?

_____

_____

_____

_____

_____

_____

5. Is it noteworthy that concupiscence (lust) entered only after the fall? What does this suggest about the nature of lust and its effect on a holy relationship with God and spouse?

_____

_____

_____

_____

_____

▶ In the Spotlight
Guardian and Protector

When Adam is placed in the Garden of Eden "to till it and keep it" (Genesis 2:15), the author was not implying that Adam was a divinely appointed landscaper. Rather, the Hebrew word used is *shamar*, which, more accurately, translates as a command "to guard" the garden—and all within it, which would eventually include the woman. The command, however, implied a forthcoming evil—Adam and Eve's disobedience and banishment from the garden. "Therefore the LORD God sent him forth from the garden of Eden, to till the ground" (Genesis 3:23). This became a necessary component of the man's vocation. Thus, the man's role as "guardian" and "protector" is woven into his manhood and the fulfillment of his vocation from the very beginning. When the man fails to protect the woman—literally and figuratively—from any and all threats, he is failing to fulfill his role as a man.

Grow!

1. Take a few minutes to ponder the feminine and masculine differences between you and your spouse. In what specific ways does a man protect his wife and family? In what specific ways does a woman nurture and care for her family? How do these two roles complement one another?

   _____

   _____

   _____

   _____

   _____

2. How did/do you decide which of you performs which duties around the house, such as cooking, paying bills, yard work, or laundry? Are these duties a product of your upbringing, societal expectations, or your own personal likes/dislikes? Are there any that you wish your spouse took more of a role in? Discuss. (Be sure to thank and affirm your partner for their work as you discuss it.)

   _____

   _____

   _____

_____

_____

3. How do you demonstrate your love to your spouse? Name three to five ways you show your spouse your love. (This could be listening to the other, serving one another, being attentive to the other's needs, affirming and encouraging him or her.) Next, ask your partner how he or she desires to be loved and what he or she may be needing from you. Listen with humility and guard against defensiveness.

_____

_____

_____

_____

_____

4. *For men*: God designed the woman in a more physiologically complex way than the man. Do you understand and consider this on a daily and monthly basis? How do you demonstrate your appreciation for that beautiful difference in design? Do you see this as a positive or negative aspect of your spouse?

For women: In what ways do you acknowledge or affirm your husband's understanding of your differences? Do you have unrealistic expectations of him to "understand" what you are feeling? How can you communicate with him in a sensitive way, while being aware of his challenge in fully comprehending what you are going through? (Be honest with one another and discuss these issues.)

_____

_____

_____

_____

_____

5. Does how you spend your free time primarily reflect "two that have become one" (see Genesis 2:24) or a relationship that is still distinctly two? How does your marriage affect your decision making when social opportunities arise? Do you consult your spouse before planning activities? Does your "guy time" or "girl time" outweigh or supersede your "couples" time? Explain why or why not.

_____

_____

_____

_____

_____

_____

▶ In the Spotlight
Celebrating Our Differences

Michelle and I [Chris] are different—very different.

I love the mornings; she prefers the nights. I think "sleeping in" is a waste of time; she thinks it's a kiss from heaven. I am logical; she is creative. I like to play any and all outdoor sports; she prefers drama and the arts. I am an introvert and drained by large groups of people; she is an extrovert and energized by social interaction. I like things to be a certain way; she is not so particular. By these standards, we would fail a compatibility test.

Did you know that there are thousands of online "compatibility tests" to help us find the "right" person and to avoid making a "big mistake"? Of the ones I have viewed, few mentioned God other than "Do you share similar views on religion?" If God is not a part of the equation, then I would agree that it is important to find someone who likes what we like, who wants what we want, or who will like us enough to let us do what we want. From this perspective, Michelle and I would never make it. We are too different, and "different" is bad.

Fortunately, there is more to the story. God knows we are different. Our differences, or complementary "gifts" as he created them to be, are intentional and "very good." God created complementary gifts unique to me as a man and to Michelle as a woman. God did not make us different to drive us apart. Rather, he created us to be unique so that together, we could experience the fullness of being created in his image. We were created for this fullness, but we must go beyond ourselves to experience it.

The reality is that Michelle and I do get annoyed with one another. We argue sometimes. We get frustrated with each other's differences. But this mainly happens when we are being selfish. "What is she doing for me?" "Why is he not loving me the way I want to be loved?" When we focus on self, we see differences. When we try to love selflessly, the same differences can turn into gifts.

Even in prayer, Michelle and I are different. I am a disciplined person at prayer. The first hour of each day is devoted to God in prayer. I work hard at my prayer life. Instead of being happy with faithfully walking with the Lord, I sometimes get frustrated that I am not making more progress. This frustration is compounded by Michelle's prayer life. She prays often but with less routine. She experiences God intimately in very short periods of time. She has a special connection to God. Sometimes I am jealous of this, but really, God is inviting me to be thankful and see it as a gift. I have the disciplined, methodical prayer life that is beautifully complemented by Michelle's less methodical but much more Spirit-led prayer. Apart we pray differently. Together we experience God more fully through prayer.

When we are focused on our differences, the result is conflict or even combat. When we celebrate what makes each other unique, we live the fullness of our marriage covenant. In the times that we allow each other to be ourselves and rejoice in our complementary gifts, we join God when he created man and woman and saw that it was "very good."

—Chris and Michelle, Tiger, Georgia

Reflect!

1. How are you uniquely suited to help your spouse grow in holiness and help him or her get to heaven?

2. Reflect on the following Scripture passages to deepen your understanding about God's plan for creation and marriage and the roles of men and women.

> When the Lord created his works from the beginning,
>   and, in making them, determined their boundaries,
> he arranged his works in an eternal order,
>   and their dominion for all generations. . . .
> Then the Lord looked upon the earth,
>   and filled it with his good things.
> With all kinds of living beings he covered its surface,
>   and into it they must return.
>
> The Lord created human beings out of earth,
>   and makes them return to it again. . . .
> He endowed them with strength like his own,
>   and made them in his own image. . . .
> Discretion and tongue and eyes,
>   ears and a mind for thinking he gave them.
> He filled them with knowledge and understanding,

and showed them good and evil.
He put the fear of him into their hearts
   to show them the majesty of his works.
(Sirach 16:26-27, 29-30; 17:1, 3, 6-8)

There is no longer Jew or Greek, there is no longer slave or free, there is no longer male and female; for all of you are one in Christ Jesus. (Galatians 3:28)

Happy the husband of a good wife;
   the number of his days will be doubled.
A loyal wife brings joy to her husband,
   and he will complete his years in peace.
A good wife is a great blessing;
   she will be granted among the blessings
      of the man who fears the Lord.
Whether rich or poor, his heart is content,
   and at all times his face is cheerful.
(Sirach 26:1-4)

But I want you to understand that Christ is the head of every man, and the husband is the head of his wife, and God is the head of Christ. . . . Indeed, man was not made from woman, but woman from man. Neither was man created for the sake of woman, but woman for the sake of man. . . . Nevertheless, in the Lord woman is not independent of man or man independent of woman. For just as woman came from man, so man comes through woman; but all things come from God. (1 Corinthians 11:3, 8-9, 11-12)

▶ In the Spotlight
Blessed John Paul II on the "Unity of the Two"

The fact that man "created as man and woman" is the image of God means not only that each of them individually is like God, as a rational and free being. It also means that man and woman, created as a "unity of the two" in their common humanity, are called to live in a communion of love, and in this way to mirror in the world the communion of love that is in God, through which the Three Persons love each other in the intimate mystery of the one divine life. . . .

In the "unity of the two," man and woman are called from the beginning not only to exist "side by side" or "together," but they are also called to exist mutually "one for the other." This also explains the meaning of the "help" spoken of in Genesis 2:18-25: "I will make him a helper fit for him." The biblical context enables us to understand this in the sense that the woman must "help" the man—and in his turn he must help her—first of all by the very fact of their "being human persons." In a certain sense this enables man and woman to discover their humanity ever anew and to confirm its whole meaning. We can easily understand that—on this fundamental level—it is a question of a "help" on the part of both, and at the same time a mutual "help." To be human means to be called to interpersonal communion. The text of Genesis 2:18-25 shows that marriage is the first and, in a sense, the fundamental dimension of this call.

—Apostolic Letter, *Mulieris Dignitatem*, 7

Act!

1. Identify three ways that you and your spouse are different. Write them down. Next, take some time to pray and find a way to genuinely affirm your spouse for each difference.

2. Make a list of things that your spouse does often but that you might not frequently stop to thank them for. Write them a note or verbally affirm them—first, for who they are, and second, for all they do.

▶ In the Spotlight
In the Image of God, Masculine and Feminine

After our third child, my husband [Paul] and I [Gretchen] decided that we desperately needed a getaway for just the two of us. With three small children close in age, we were finding it hard to connect the way we used to. When a friend offered for us to use her lake house, we jumped at the opportunity! We brought the kids to my parents' house and headed out of town to spend some much needed time alone together.

On one of the days, we decided to go on a bike ride on a wooded trail that was a couple of miles long. I was so excited to have this time with my husband, sharing this adventure together. My excitement quickly turned to disappointment, however, when I realized that we had two very different visions of how this bike-ride excursion would go. At first we rode in tandem. But at some point, he began racing ahead and then would stop to wait for me when he noticed I hadn't caught up to his breakneck speed. This continued until we arrived back to our car. My expectation for this bike ride had been to take our time and enjoy the scenery, and to stop on occasion and sit by the creek and "talk." My beloved, on the other hand, wanted to *conquer* the trail!

I learned a lot that day, especially after we were able to discuss the whole thing. I was reminded that my husband has a "challenge and conquer" mentality, as do most men. He was created by God to be more "wild at heart." My feminine heart is wired to be more relational. I think this dichotomy was evident on the bike trail that day in my desire to talk and in his desire to finish that trail strong.

When he and I take the time to understand where the other person is coming from, appreciate each other's uniqueness, and, at times, compromise to love each other selflessly, God is glorified. Our differences are meant to complement one another and bless our friendship and marital union, to help us breathe with both lungs. The "two becoming one flesh" does not mean that my husband is supposed to morph into looking just like me or that I am supposed to morph into looking just like him. We are called to be who God created us to be in our masculinity and femininity and together mirror to the world God's image and his great love for his bride, the Church.

Although there are still differences as male and female that trip us up at times, we rely on God's grace to fill us with humility and acceptance, to provide good communication, to help us be patient with one another, and to simply make it a priority to love. St. Paul, in his letter to the Ephesians, sums it up when he writes, "Rather, living the truth in love, we should grow in every way into him who is the head, Christ, from whom the whole body, joined and held together by every supporting ligament, with the proper functioning of each part, brings about the body's growth and builds itself up in love" (4:15-16, NAB).

—Gretchen and Paul, Houma, Louisiana

It Takes Three to Be Married

Ecclesiastes 4:7-12

[7]Again, I saw vanity under the sun: [8]the case of solitary individuals, without sons or brothers; yet there is no end to all their toil, and their eyes are never satisfied with riches. "For whom am I toiling," they ask, "and depriving myself of pleasure?" This also is vanity and an unhappy business.

> Happiness is to be found in the home where God is loved and honored, where each one loves, and helps, and cares for the others.
> —St. Theophane Venard

[9]Two are better than one, because they have a good reward for their toil. [10]For if they fall, one will lift up the other; but woe to one who is alone and falls and does not have another to help. [11]Again, if two lie together, they keep warm; but how can one keep warm alone? [12]And though one might prevail against another, two will withstand one. A threefold cord is not quickly broken.

Ecclesiastes is a very unique book in that it doesn't speak *to* God but merely *about* God. The author never addresses God directly, nor does God ever speak to the writer. The entire book is a wrestling match between the mind and the heart of the author, who calls himself "Teacher" (Ecclesiastes 1:1).

Ecclesiastes portrays the author's internal struggle between hope and hopelessness. This Teacher wonders if this world really has any redeeming value in it, any true beauty or love. Does it possess anything that's not wholly or inherently fleeting? The word "vanity" is used well over two dozen times in Ecclesiastes' twelve short chapters. In this context, vanity is not to be confused strictly with pride or an obsession with one's looks. In using this word, the writer is speaking more about emptiness—fittingly so, since "vanity" is derived from the Latin root *vanus*, which means "empty."

Though Ecclesiastes was probably penned around 950 B.C., even a cursory glance at the book and the answers it seeks demonstrates that not much has changed in three thousand years. Countless souls still struggle with these same questions about whether God is truly present in their lives. Is God the loving Father, active and available, or is he the absentee Father, who spins us into creation and then abandons us as infants, orphaning us in a cruel and sin-filled world?

In this passage the reader is given a glimmer of hope. God just might be closer than the author originally believed. These verses show us the possibility of life's meaning by pointing out our loneliness and our innate desire to share our lives (and even our beds) with another.

However, the love perceived and "shared" seems far more practical than conjugal. Two bodies will get more work done (Ecclesiastes 4:9) and stay warmer on cold nights (4:11). It's efficient, it's pragmatic, it's utilitarian, but there's a hint of something more. Here, as in various other places within Ecclesiastes, there is a faint ray of sunlight that might just fill the chasm of emptiness so apparent in the mind and heart of the author. The author of Ecclesiastes hints at, but never learns, that love is the point, the "meaning" of life.

This passage is especially challenging to the modern workaholic mentality. Countless marriages are in shambles and many spouses feel emotionally divorced due to the vanity-ridden pursuit of money. The constant desire to gain greater financial security, to virtually "widow" one's spouse season after season until the next project is done or the next promotion is finalized, is, as the author reminds us, rooted in emptiness. In the end, it's all vanity.

The timeless wisdom of this passage is of fundamental importance to a healthy, happy marriage in the modern world. Choose relationship over riches (Ecclesiastes 4:8). Learn when to say, "Enough is enough." There's a reason for the cliché that it's lonely at the top. To get there usually means abandoning those whom we say we're doing it for in the first place. In the end, if we hold on to worldly wealth or our jobs with two hands, we won't have a hand to join to the hand of our spouse. We won't have two arms available to embrace our spouse at the end of a tiring work day. The practical questions advanced in this passage speak to priorities and motivations.

Do you ever feel alone or abandoned? Do you question God's presence during difficult times, such as financial hardships or deaths, or in bouts of depression, stress, or anxiety? If so, to whom do you lean into for comfort and warmth in such times? (Ecclesiastes 4:11). To your spouse? To God? Both, hopefully, because a successful marriage takes three: the man, the woman, and God. As we are reminded, "A threefold cord is not quickly broken" (4:12).

> Countless souls still struggle with these same questions about whether God is truly present in their lives.

You cannot quiet your restless heart without knowing God. Similarly, you cannot have a truly blessed, joyful, grace-filled, sacramental marriage without knowing God and inviting him to be the foundation upon which you build your lives together.

Understand!

1. Read the passage from Ecclesiastes and substitute the word "emptiness" for "vanity." Why is an understanding of vanity's true meaning so vital to fully comprehending this passage? In what ways in your life have you sought "vanities" but come up empty?

   _____

   _____

   _____

_____

_____

_____

2. Read Ecclesiastes 2:1-11. What other things did the writer discover were "vanities"? Why do human beings never seem satisfied with earthly things? Why is there a seemingly inherent need for more? How is this struggle seen today?

_____

_____

_____

_____

_____

_____

3. In this passage, how does the partnership of the two people affect their work? How does their work affect their relationship? In your own life, how does your work affect your marriage and how does your marriage affect your work? Be specific.

_____

_____

_____

_____

_____

_____

4. What is the difference between people living as partners (splitting tasks and duties) and an actual intimate partnership? In what ways does the writer of this passage show that the partnership is more than one of just strictly splitting the daily workload?

_____

_____

_____

_____

_____

_____

_____

5. Why is the analogy of a three-ply cord an apt one to describe a marriage with God as its center? Would other people see your marriage as a three-ply cord? Why or why not?

_____

_____

_____

_____

_____

_____

▶ In the Spotlight
The Bible's Only Book of Philosophy

The Book of Ecclesiastes is called "Qoheleth" in the Hebrew Bible, which means "preacher." When the Old Testament was translated into Greek, the name "Ekklesiastes" was given to it (*ekklesia* is the word for "assembly" or "church"). Because the author is called "the son of David, king in Jerusalem" (Ecclesiastes 1:1), it was commonly believed to have been written by King Solomon, son of David and Bathsheba, who was unmatched in wisdom (1 Kings 4:29). While some scholars debate Solomon's authorship, what is clear is that the writer is on a mission—seeking truth about life and its meaning. Here is how one Scripture commentator describes this book:

> [Ecclesiastes] is the Bible's only book of philosophy. Philosophy is the wisdom of human reason alone, without any appeal to divine revelation. [Ecclesiastes] exposes the deepest need of the human heart with ruthless honesty. This

book is tremendously valuable for us, even though it begins and ends in despair. Ecclesiastes highlights the problem; Christ is the answer. (Peter Kreeft, *You Can Understand the Bible*)

Grow!

1. How often are you there for your spouse in ways that really count? How often do work or other responsibilities take you away from time with your spouse and family? If it's more often than either of you desire, what could you do to change it?

_____

_____

_____

_____

_____

_____

2. How does God fill the emptiness in our lives? When have you felt empty, and when has God been able to fill you up?

_____

_____

_____

_____

_____

_____

3. In what ways do you make God the center of your relationship with your spouse? How would the nurturing of a personal relationship

with Christ on an individual basis help to unify you as a couple so that you become a "threefold cord" (Ecclesiastes 4:12)?

_____

_____

_____

_____

_____

_____

4. Do you believe that God speaks and works through your spouse to help you achieve holiness and ultimately sainthood? If your spouse is calling you to change, do you see it as God calling you to it or merely as a form of manipulation from the other? Discuss.

_____

_____

_____

_____

_____

_____

5. Our daily conversations say a lot about the state of our relationships and whether we view our spouses as true partners. Are your conversations more positive than negative? Do your words lift one another up rather than tear one another down? Do they reflect a sense of working together or of working at cross purposes? Explain and discuss.

_____

_____

_____

_____

_____

_____

▶ In the Spotlight
It Takes Three to Make Love

The basic error of mankind has been to assume that only two are needed for love: you and me, or society and me, or humanity and me. Really, it takes three: self, other selves, and God; you, and me, and God. Love of self without love of God is selfishness; love of neighbor without love of God embraces only those who are pleasing to us, not those who are hateful. One cannot tie two sticks together without something outside the sticks. . . . Duality in love is extinction through the exhaustion of self-giving.

It takes three to make love. What binds lover and beloved together on earth is an ideal outside both. As it is impossible to have rain without clouds, so it is impossible to understand love without God. If we would seek out the mystery of why love has a triune character and implies lover, beloved, and love, we must mount to God Himself. The ultimate reason it takes three to make love is that God is Love, and His Love is Triune.

—Archbishop Fulton Sheen, *Three to Get Married*

Reflect!

1. How much importance do you place on worldly things in your marriage? What drives you? In what or in whom do you trust?

2. Reflect on the following Scripture passages about making God the first priority in our lives and in our marriages:

Then the LORD God said, "It is not good that the man should be alone; I will make him a helper as his partner." (Genesis 2:18)

Now if you are unwilling to serve the LORD, choose this day whom you will serve, whether the gods your ancestors served in the region beyond the River or the gods of the Amorites in whose land you are living; but as for me and my household, we will serve the LORD. (Joshua 24:15)

[Jesus said,] "But strive first for the kingdom of God and his righteousness, and all these things will be given to you as well." (Matthew 6:33)

But those who want to be rich fall into temptation and are trapped by many senseless and harmful desires that plunge people into ruin and destruction. For the love of money is a root of all kinds of evil, and in their eagerness to be rich some have wandered away from the faith and pierced themselves with many pains. . . .

As for those who in the present age are rich, command them not to be haughty, or to set their hopes on the uncertainty of riches, but rather on God who richly provides us with everything for our enjoyment. They are to do good, to be rich in good works, generous, and ready to share. (1 Timothy 6:9-10, 17-18)

Like good stewards of the manifold grace of God, serve one another with whatever gift each of you has received. (1 Peter 4:10)

▶ In the Spotlight
The Sacramental Nature of Marriage

Authentic married love is caught up into divine love and is governed and enriched by Christ's redeeming power and the saving activity of the Church, so that this love may lead the spouses to God with powerful effect and may aid and strengthen them in sublime office of being a father or a mother. For this reason

Christian spouses have a special sacrament by which they are fortified and receive a kind of consecration in the duties and dignity of their state. By virtue of this sacrament, as spouses fulfill their conjugal and family obligation, they are penetrated with the spirit of Christ, which suffuses their whole lives with faith, hope, and charity. Thus they increasingly advance the perfection of their own personalities, as well as their mutual sanctification, and hence contribute jointly to the glory of God.

—Second Vatican Council, *Gaudium et Spes*, 48

For Christians, marriage is a sacrament and you may almost say that for Christians it is the sacrament par excellence . . . in the sense that it helps us, more than any of the others, to understand what the word "sacrament" means. Matrimony is the only sacrament which is called a sacrament in the Bible. A man will leave his father and mother, St. Paul says to the Ephesians, and will cling to his wife, and the two will become one flesh. Yes, those words are a high mystery—*sacramentum*, of course, is just a token-word used to represent the Greek *musterion*. Because, define the word "sacrament" how you will, the root idea of it is clearly this, that something purely spiritual and something purely physical are presented close side by side. And in human marriage, even when it involves no shred of religious observance, that dual character hits you in the face. Love, which is the most spiritual thing given in our experience outside of religion, is there side by side with the satisfaction of a purely physical desire; the angel in us and the animal in us are both at work, and not as contrasts or opposites. Spiritual aspiration finds its expression in, and is fostered by, the brute facts of biology.

—Fr. Ronald Knox, *The Hidden Stream: Mysteries of the Christian Faith*

Act!

1. Create a time to pray together every day. Vary the forms of prayer. You could start off simply by praying an Our Father, Hail Mary, and Glory Be, or a decade of the Rosary. Express your prayer intentions for yourselves, your marriage, and your children and family members. Perhaps you could go once a week to adoration together, or make a date to go to confession and then out for coffee afterward. If your schedule permits, attend Mass together during the week.

2. Create a prayer room, corner, or space in your home or yard. Work on it together.

▶ In the Spotlight
Our True Foundation

I [Darren] was shocked one day to receive a call from my wife [Bobbi] informing me that our house was on fire. She had called 911, and the kids were safe. I left the office, jumped in my car, and rushed home. It took only fifteen minutes, but it seemed like forever. Were our pets inside? What about our wedding pictures? Almost everything we owned was in that house. Did we lose everything?

My stomach dropped as I saw that the police had blocked off our entire neighborhood. I left the car on the side of the road and ran the last few blocks. Fortunately, when I arrived, the fire was out and the house was still standing. I had a moment of true thanksgiving to God for his generosity. I was told that one of our dogs did not make it out. I was already thinking about how I would tell my daughter when the dog came running out the front door, to the cheers of all the neighbors.

After hours of waiting, they allowed us in to view our home. The fire had started in the kitchen, which was destroyed, but the fire department had put out the fire before it did any structural damage—another moment of thanksgiving. However, I learned that day of the tremendous damage that smoke can cause. Almost everything in the house was lost.

As the sun set on the day, we realized that we had nothing but the clothes on our backs. At 8 p.m. we were in Target, buying everything from toothbrushes to clothes for school the next day. Our comfortable life had been turned upside down. With the kids finally tucked in at a hotel, reality really set in. Where were we going to live? How were we going to afford this? My wife and I realized that we had to answer a simple question— one that before this day we thought we knew the answer to: Did we truly trust God?

Together, hand-in-hand, we answered that question. We were committed to each other and to God, and we were committed to being an example to our children about what is truly important in life. What could separate us from the love of God? Surely not a house fire. This event brought renewal in our marital relationship and in our faith life. Immediately the blessings started pouring in. We never lacked for a place to sleep, something to eat, or a helping hand.

Our insurance kicked in and took care of the finances, but what really made the difference was our marital insurance policy. So many years before this event, we had professed our vows: for better or for worse, for richer or for poorer. We meant those words and had done our best to live them out daily. Our marital journey began with a man and a woman who loved each other and who also loved God. How generous our Lord is to remind us that after twenty years of marriage, the foundation of our family is simply two people in love with each other and with God! "The rain fell, the floods came, and the winds blew and beat on that house, but it did not fall, because it had been founded on rock" (Matthew 7:25).

—Darren and Bobbi, Mesa, Arizona

When the Soul
Leads the Body

1 Corinthians 6:15-20; 7:1-5, 8-11

6:15Do you not know that your bodies are members of Christ? Should I therefore take the members of Christ and make them members of a prostitute? Never! 16Do you not know that whoever is united to a prostitute becomes one body with her? For it is said, "The two shall be one flesh." 17But anyone united to the Lord becomes one spirit with him. 18Shun fornication! Every sin that a person commits is outside the body; but the fornicator sins against the body itself. 19Or do you not know that your body is a temple of the Holy Spirit within you, which you have from God, and that you are not your own? 20For you were bought with a price; therefore glorify God in your body.

> Purity prepares the soul for love, and love confirms the soul in purity.
>
> —Blessed John Henry Newman

7:1Now concerning the matters about which you wrote: "It is well for a man not to touch a woman." 2But because of cases of sexual immorality, each man should have his own wife and each woman her own husband. 3The husband should give to his wife her conjugal rights, and likewise the wife to her husband. 4For the wife does not have authority over her own body, but the husband does; likewise the husband does not have authority over his own body, but the wife does. 5Do not deprive one another except perhaps by agreement for a set time, to devote yourselves to prayer, and then come together again, so that Satan may not tempt you because of your lack of self-control. . . .

8To the unmarried and the widows I say that it is well for them to remain unmarried as I am. 9But if they are not practicing self-control, they should marry. For it is better to marry than to be aflame with passion.

10To the married I give this command—not I but the Lord—that the wife should not separate from her husband 11(but if she does separate, let her remain unmarried or else be reconciled to her husband), and that the husband should not divorce his wife.

A ncient Corinth would make modern-day Las Vegas look tame by comparison. Lying on the coast of the Mediterranean Sea about sixty miles southwest of Athens, Corinth was a metropolis in ancient Greece. A seaport town, Corinth was a strategic commercial hub for constant trade, but amid the bevy of importing and exporting, Corinth was known for its rampant sinfulness. One scholar described it this way:

> Corinth was the largest, most cosmopolitan, and most decadent city in Greece. Two-thirds of its seven hundred thousand citizens were slaves. It was a major port and hub of commerce. Much of the commerce was in human flesh. Men went to Corinth to take a moral holiday. The city was full of idolatry, which centered around Aphrodite, the goddess of sex. Her temple, atop an eighteen-hundred-foot promontory, had a thousand temple prostitutes. (Peter Kreeft, *You Can Understand the Bible*)

St. Paul arrived in Corinth as part of his second missionary journey, most likely sometime between 50–53 A.D. He had helped to start the church in Corinth, living among the Corinthians for eighteen months (Acts 18:11), but he was unable to remain in the city and oversee its spiritual growth (18:12-18). Unfortunately, a lot of scandalous behavior began to emerge within the community in Corinth after the apostle left. Through word of mouth, St. Paul heard about some of the sins that the Christians had been committing. In this letter, he was writing to encourage them to reject their immoral behavior and renew their commitment to a life grounded in the love of Christ (1 Corinthians 10:6-13).

Living among the people, preaching in the Corinthian streets, St. Paul no doubt saw his share of sin, including the enormous temple dedicated to Aphrodite and the temple prostitutes. Religious prostitution was an accepted part of pagan culture. Paul uses the analogy of prostitution (1 Corinthians 6:15-16) to make the point that shunning sexual immorality (6:18) is the equivalent of shunning idolatry. Remember, the temple was dedicated to a false god.

Beyond the obvious allusion, however, there is a deeper warning for the fallen soul. Sex is from God, but it can never take the place of God, especially not in marriage. Although a celibate single, St. Paul knew well the temptations of the flesh. He warns us to take a pro-active approach in shunning any and all situations or environments that might unleash lust or vanquish virtue (1 Corinthians 7:1-2). As Blessed John Paul II reminds us, the opposite of love is not hate; the opposite of love is use. We cannot measure our holiness by the holiness (or lack thereof) of those around us, especially those who do not believe what we proclaim to believe. We belong to Christ. We are members of Christ's body. (For a more in-depth unpacking of what it means to be "members of Christ," it is wise to spend ample time reflecting on 1 Corinthians 12:12-31.) These are not philosophical ideas that St. Paul is advancing to us; these are real struggles that we face, with real souls on the line.

> Sex is from God, but it can never take the place of God.

Imagine St. Paul standing upon those stairs looking into the eyes of sinners—both women and men—and proclaiming this eternal truth: "Your body is a temple of the Holy Spirit within you" (1 Corinthians 6:19). In other words, while facing and pointing to Aphrodite's palace of iniquity, the great saint was proclaiming, "This is not a temple; *you* are." We are being called to "glorify God in [our] body" (6:20). Unlike the pagans of the time, who glorified gods in temples of prostitution and orgies, we are called to honor the one true God in the temples of our own bodies. When it comes to authentic worship, we might proclaim who God is and who we are with our lips, but in reality, we proclaim who God is and whose we are with our bodies. When sex is separated from the sacramental/covenantal bonds of marriage, its purpose is lost, and the result is selfishness; it is mere use. And since our body is a temple of God, misusing it is an act of desecration and profanation.

Later in 1 Corinthians, we are reminded that "if [we] speak in the tongues of mortals and of angels, but do not have love, [we are] a noisy gong or a clanging cymbal" (13:1). Simply put, without love— true sacrificial love—sex is just noise and a hollow echo of what the Lord intended the physical act to be and to usher forth: life and self-less love.

It's in this transition into chapter seven too that we are reminded of the indissolubility of marriage, as St. Paul gives practical advice regarding the permanence and sanctity of marriage. In saying "not I but the Lord" (1 Corinthians 7:10), he echoes Christ's warning against divorce (Mark 10:2-12). Divorce is not an option, according to Paul; couples must either "remain unmarried or else be reconciled" (1 Corinthians 7:10). This is the scriptural basis, again, for why the Church does not honor divorce as an option. It comes from Christ and was observed throughout the early Church.

In this letter we see, not only how understanding and sensitive St. Paul is to human weakness and temptation (1 Corinthians 7:9), but also how practical and pastoral he is in showing us how to overcome it. His sage advice is quite direct in how to interact with one another, how to avoid sin, and how to cooperate with God's grace. In his Letter to the Romans, St. Paul deepens our understanding of this point even further, noting that the flesh and the spirit are constantly at odds with each other (see Romans 6–8 in particular). While God gifts us with our bodies to honor him and all of creation, our flesh (body) often leads our spirit (soul) away from the light of God and into the slavery of sin.

While the body and soul are intrinsically linked and created to work in unison through God's grace, sin hampers that perfect union. St. Paul addresses this eternal tug-of-war between body and soul in a very practical way in the First Letter to the Corinthians. This battle is not to be taken lightly. Our bodies are gifts to one another, never to be degraded, discarded, or used. Paul forcefully and passionately reminds the Corinthians—and us, two thousand years later—of this timeless truth: Everything we have, even our bodies, belongs to Christ. He emphatically calls us all to respond, in virtue, to the struggles that accompany marriage and the Christian life. Like a strong father, St. Paul is lovingly firm in his guidance and unrelenting in his resolve.

Understand!

1. Why do you think St. Paul so strongly desired that the church in Corinth see the link between flesh and spirit, body and soul? How was his thinking so different from the pagan philosophy of the day?

_____

_____

_____

_____

_____

2. When you read, "Your body is a temple of the Holy Spirit within you" (1 Corinthians 6:19), what is your response? How do you think the Corinthians reacted? Do you see this more as a philosophical reality than a spiritual or physical one? Why or why not?

_____

_____

_____

_____

_____

3. What does 1 Corinthians 7:9 teach us about the dangers and reality of sexual temptation? About self-control? How does being able to say no to temptations make the things we say yes to so much more significant? How does something like pornography demonstrate this truth?

_____

_____

_____

_____

_____

4. Why does St. Paul, a celibate, speak so strongly about the importance of a holy marriage and the indissolubility of it? Why is his perspective on the matter so important?

_____

_____

_____

_____

_____

5. In what ways is the sinful "Corinthian spirit" still alive and at work in our culture today? In what ways has sex been separated from God and its spiritual component?

_____

_____

_____

_____

_____

_____

▶ In the Spotlight: What Is Profane?

The term "profanity" comes from the Latin term *profanes*, and its etymology is quite interesting, given St. Paul's teaching on the body as the "temple of the Holy Spirit" (1 Corinthians 6:19). The word is a combination of *pro* (which means "before" or "outside of") and *fanum* (which is the Latin word for "temple"). So quite literally, the word "profanity" refers to things that belong outside of the temple—things that are not sacred. Later in 1 Corinthians, St. Paul warns the members of the community not to partake in the Eucharist if they are not properly disposed to do so (11:27-29). Additionally, in his Letter to the Ephesians, he warns the young church to be on guard against profane speech (4:29). For St. Paul, no profane word or deed could be allowed from a Christian, for we are temples of the Holy Spirit.

Grow!

1. In your own words, what does sex mean to you in your marriage? Do you look at sex as more of a gift of self or a gift *to* yourself? Is your attitude more of "give" or "take"? Each spouse should take a moment to explain and discuss.

   _____

   _____

   _____

   _____

   _____

2. What steps do you take—if any—to insure that your sexual encounters are not lustful or strictly self-serving? Do you see your spouse's body as something to be lusted after or admired? Do you view your spouse as just a "body" in the sexual encounter? Is pornography present anywhere in the relationship?

_____

_____

_____

_____

_____

_____

3. How do you insure that your lines of communication are open and honest, including issues about sex? Are you open to your spouse's counsel and insight? Are you aware of any insecurities or struggles? Are there topics you refuse to talk about in detail? Be honest and take the time to discuss these issues.

_____

_____

_____

_____

_____

_____

4. What are some ways in which you have failed to treat your body as a "temple"? Does your sexual past (or your spouse's) ever leave you concerned about your marital future? Is there anything your spouse could do to help you "reconsecrate" the temple of your body to God?

_____

_____

_____

_____

5. Do you take time to embrace one another and show affection before expressing your love sexually? How do you create intimacy in your marriage beyond the sexual act? What would your spouse want you to do to create a greater sense of intimacy?

_____

_____

_____

_____

_____

_____

▶ In the Spotlight
How to Conquer Lust

The most important thing to know about lust is how to avoid it. Since it is the most popular sin, both the most attractive and the most widespread, any workable advice on overcoming it would seem pretty rare and valuable. . . . Only when we are truly humble does God give us the grace to conquer lust. God is not a substitute for sex, as Freud thought; sex is often a substitute for God. The deepest passion of the soul is meant for God. When the true God comes, the false gods go. To conquer lust, forget about lust and love God.

—Peter Kreeft, *Back to Virtue*

It is clear that in Matthew 5:27-28, Christ demanded detachment from the evil of lust (or of the look of disorderly desire). . . . The accusation leveled at the evil of lust is at the same time an appeal to overcome it. . . . As we know, Christ said: "Everyone who looks at a woman lustfully has already committed adultery with her in his heart." Adultery committed in the heart can and must be understood as "devaluation," or as the impoverishment of an authentic value. It is an intentional deprivation of that dignity to which the complete value of her femininity corresponds in the person in question. Matthew 5:27-28 contains a call to discover this value and this dignity, and to reassert them.

The appeal to master the lust of the flesh springs precisely from the affirmation of the personal dignity of the body and of sex, and serves only this dignity.

—Blessed John Paul II, *Theology of the Body* Audience, October 22, 1980

Reflect!

1. With divorce so prevalent in our culture, what proof or hope do you give your spouse that you are in it for the long haul? How do you show your spouse—daily—how primary he or she is to you? Give tangible examples.

2. Reflect on the following Scripture passages about the tug-of-war between the body and the spirit:

Now the works of the flesh are obvious: fornication, impurity, licentiousness, idolatry, sorcery, enmities, strife, jealousy, anger, quarrels, dissensions, factions, envy, drunkenness, carousing, and things like these. I am warning you, as I warned you before: those who do such things will not inherit the kingdom of God. (Galatians 5:19-21)

I appeal to you therefore, brothers and sisters, by the mercies of God, to present your bodies as a living sacrifice, holy and acceptable to God, which is your spiritual worship. Do not be conformed to this world, but be transformed by the renewing of your minds, so that you may discern what is the will of God—what is good and acceptable and perfect. (Romans 12:1-2)

All that is in the world—the desire of the flesh, the desire of the eyes, the pride in riches—comes not from the Father but from the world. And the world and its desire are passing away, but those who do the will of God live forever. (1 John 2:16-17)

[Jesus said,] "But I say to you that everyone who looks at a woman with lust has already committed adultery with her in his heart." (Matthew 5:28)

Let marriage be held in honor by all, and let the marriage bed be kept undefiled; for God will judge fornicators and adulterers. (Hebrews 13:4)

▶ In the Spotlight
Creating and Sustaining Intimacy

Intimacy is a very important part of every healthy marriage. For a marriage to be successful, a couple must find the time and make the effort to nourish the relationship. When I [Paul] was first married, I used to get together with an older married guy every now and then, and we would talk about life. Ultimately, the conversation would always be driven by my asking him questions about marriage. I can remember telling him during one of these conversations that my wife [Gretchen] had been questioning how much I loved her. He asked me, "When was the last time you told her you loved her?" I responded, "I told her yesterday that I loved her." To which he replied, "Unless you tell her and show her every day, she will always wonder if there is someone or something else that you love more."

This statement made a huge impact on me. Saying "I do" at the wedding is only the beginning. Saying "I love you" every day is essential. For true, authentic intimacy to be a part of your marriage, you have to make a commitment and effort to share your heart and soul with your spouse on an ongoing basis. When my wife and I make this effort in our marriage, it pays off. We both feel loved, we both feel connected to one another, and we both are able to keep our eyes focused on what's most important: Jesus and our marital love. Here are three things that we have learned in our marriage that have kept intimacy alive in our relationship and protected our married sexuality from the lies of the world:

We are a gift that keeps on giving. God created us male and female as a gift to be given and shared with each other. My wife and I experience the greatest intimacy in our marriage when we give ourselves unselfishly to each other. This can happen in many different ways: during sex, when we are talking, when we are serving. When we seek intimacy for our own selfish desires, we will often find that our spouse will react negatively by pulling back from us. We are a gift created to give and not take, and we find ultimate fulfillment when we love in this way.

Effort goes a long way in loving your spouse. We all know the saying, "Actions speak louder than words." This is so true for marriage! My wife and I are busy with work, kids, life—just like everyone else. But we have decided that although romance isn't always going to be a candlelight dinner, we need to make an effort to love the other person each day. My effort, even though it may be small, shows my spouse how much I love her.

For your eyes only. In a world that is soaked with sexual temptations, it's important that you help protect each other's dignity. Intimacy between husband and wife is much greater when your heart and eyes are focused on the other person. It's important to weed out any temptations, distractions, or negative behaviors that detract from seeing yourself and your spouse with the utmost dignity, beauty, and love. My wife and I have total access into each other's lives so that we can help one another stay pure. We don't hide our computers, phones, relationships with others, or work. Everything is open to one another so that we have loving accountability and so that we can help each other stay faithful in all ways.

—Paul and Gretchen, Houma, Louisiana

Act!

1. Make it a point—every night—to bless one another before bed. Use holy water, if possible, and take a few moments to make it an intimate way to invite God into your bedroom and end the day prayerfully.

2. Protect one another's dignity with the media you take in. Vow to turn off any movies or television shows that debase the human body and sexuality or contain profanity.

3. Recognize that foreplay begins outside the bedroom. Offer one another massages and back rubs and foot rubs. Do random acts of service around the house, cleaning or picking up. Surprise the other by coming home early from work to get the laundry done.

▶ In the Spotlight
The Saints on Purity and Fidelity

Humility is the safeguard of chastity. In the matter of purity, there is no greater danger than not fearing danger. When a person puts himself in an occasion, saying, "I shall not fall," it is an almost infallible sign that he will fall, and with great injury to his soul. —St. Philip Neri

Purity? they ask—and they smile. They are the very people who approach marriage with worn-out bodies and disillusioned minds. —St. Josémaria Escrivá

To be pure, to remain pure, can only come at a price, the price of knowing God and loving him enough to do his will. He will always give us the strength we need to keep purity as something beautiful for him. —Blessed Mother Teresa

The person who does not decide to love forever will find it very difficult to really love for even one day. —Blessed John Paul II

Dying to Ourselves

Ephesians 5:21-33

²¹Be subject to one another out of reverence for Christ.

²²Wives, be subject to your husbands as you are to the Lord. ²³For the husband is the head of the wife just as Christ is the head of the church, the body of which he is the Savior. ²⁴Just as the church is subject to Christ, so also wives ought to be, in everything, to their husbands.

> The "great mystery," which is the Church and humanity in Christ, does not exist apart from the "great mystery" expressed in the "one flesh" . . . [the] reality of marriage and the family.
> —Blessed John Paul II

²⁵Husbands, love your wives, just as Christ loved the church and gave himself up for her, ²⁶in order to make her holy by cleansing her with the washing of water by the word, ²⁷so as to present the church to himself in splendor, without a spot or wrinkle or anything of the kind—yes, so that she may be holy and without blemish. ²⁸In the same way, husbands should love their wives as they do their own bodies. He who loves his wife loves himself. ²⁹For no one ever hates his own body, but he nourishes and tenderly cares for it, just as Christ does for the church, ³⁰because we are members of his body. ³¹"For this reason a man will leave his father and mother and be joined to his wife, and the two will become one flesh." ³²This is a great mystery, and I am applying it to Christ and the church. ³³Each of you, however, should love his wife as himself, and a wife should respect her husband.

S t. Paul most likely wrote this letter during one of his stints in prison. There is a beautiful irony in the fact that while he sits alone, separated from the greater Church and her worship, he writes of the great interconnectedness of the body of Christ. His Letter to the Ephesians is all about relationships—earthly and heavenly, matrimonial and mystical. We aren't just members of an organization; we are members of a body. We are organs and muscles and appendages, vital to one another's sustenance and survival. The body of Christ is made up of living, breathing members (1 Corinthians 12:27; Ephesians 4:12)—of sinners seeking sanctity, not of saints who boast of it.

In this letter, St. Paul focuses all of his energy on helping the young church in Ephesus understand what being "members of his body" (Ephesians 5:30) really means. The reality of being part of Christ's very body—living and breathing and organic—has both personal and communal implications. It's also a mystical reality, beyond the comprehension of our own eyes and sensibilities. This is not a "quick sell" concept that St. Paul is forwarding to the community of believers. This is a new way of thinking and living. Jesus Christ raised the stakes by raising the dignity of the human person and the way in which that person is called to live and lay down this life. As we said in the introduction, the mystery of our lives in Christ is not so much one to be *solved* as one to *behold*. St. Paul tells us directly, "This is a great mystery" (5:32). We must be willing to look beyond the modern and earthly understanding of the words and behold the mystical, heavenly truths breathed forth by the Holy Spirit in this passage.

To be "subject to one another" (Ephesians 5:21) calls for a unified love, in which the husband and wife become one in more ways than just sexually; this subjection is voluntary, mutual, and reciprocal. The selfless love of the husband for his wife is supposed to reveal and model the selfless love of Christ (the bridegroom) for the Church (the bride) (5:25-27). Quite literally, the "mission" of the man is to die for his bride as Christ did for the Church.

And what is the woman's role? In a complete contradiction to ancient thinking, which often regarded the wife as far lower or even the property of the man, St. Paul is offering a new image. It is one that recognizes and honors the dignity of the woman, just as Christ did (John 4:7-42) and as St. Paul echoes in other writings (Galatians 3:28). The woman's role is to be "under" the mission (sub-mission) of the man. The bride must acquiesce by allowing the man to lay down his life for her. As she entrusts herself to her husband, she is, by extension, entrusting herself to Christ and honoring the Lord.

The "washing" mentioned (Ephesians 5:26) is intended to remind us of our baptism, when we became a new creation through the sanctifying action of Jesus the Bridegroom. The Church (the Bride), presented "in splendor, . . . holy and without blemish" (5:27), is an allusion to a customary Jewish marital practice in which the bride washed and dressed herself before being presented to her husband.

> How far am I willing to go for a strong marriage?

The apostle's wordplay likening the man's flesh to his wife (Ephesians 5:29) points us back to the creation story of Genesis (2:24), insuring that we see the connection to God's original plan of sacrificial love and of the two becoming one flesh (Ephesians 5:31). A husband must be willing to "die" for his bride, as evidenced in Jesus, the New Adam. In Eden self-preservation took precedence over self-sacrifice; Adam and Eve were unwilling to "die" to their own desires for the Creator who had given them everything. Are we?

On a practical, daily basis, what does this subjection and "sub-mission" look like? To find out, we have to ask ourselves these questions: How well do I die to my own wants and needs? How far am I willing to go for a strong marriage? Am I really willing to sacrifice—in big and small ways—for my spouse? Am I willing to yield to my spouse when necessary?

We can be married but not act as if we are married—and it's our actions, more than just our words or any symbols, that count. Christ's identity and kingship were made known not by the sign above his head on the cross but by the fact that he freely gave up his life for us. It was his sacrifice that made him king. Likewise, it's not our tax return, our address label, or even the wedding band on our finger that make us married. It's how we decide to lay down our lives for one another that makes us truly one in Christ and one with each other.

As St. Paul so eloquently states in this passage, marriage is a profound mystery, one that reveals the love of Christ for his Church (Ephesians 5:32). Marriage is about sacrifice, about "death to self" so that the other might live. It calls us to abandon all preconceived notions of what will and ought to make us happy, and to embrace all that comes with each passing day. Maybe we feel entitled to a certain level of happiness or material prosperity in our marriage and get angry at God if that doesn't happen. But in God's plan for marriage, the more we give of ourselves, the more we receive and the happier we become. Sacrifice is the key to our unity—two becoming one flesh.

Understand!

1. This passage is often referred to as the "elbow verse"—when wives dig their elbows into their husbands' ribs as it is read at Mass. What has been your reaction in the past to this passage? What is it now? Is the idea of "submission" still a stumbling block for you?

_____

_____

_____

_____

_____

2. Why is "death to self" necessary for the "two to become one"? How does St. Paul explain the concept in this passage?

_____

_____

_____

_____

_____

_____

3. How do we show reverence for Christ when we subject ourselves to one another (Ephesians 6:21)? How does this honor the Lord?

_____

_____

_____

_____

_____

_____

4. Have you ever thought of Christ dying for you so that he could cleanse you and present you without a blemish of any kind (Ephesians 5:27)? What other images in this passage especially speak to you?

_____

_____

_____

_____

_____

_____

5. Put into your own words what St. Paul meant when he instructed the man to love his wife as "himself" (Ephesians 5:28). Put into your own words what he meant when he instructed the woman to "respect her husband" (5:33).

_____

_____

_____

_____

_____

_____

▶ In the Spotlight:
Love Excludes Domination

[St. Paul] does not intend to say that the husband is the lord of the wife and that the interpersonal pact proper to marriage is a pact of domination of the husband over the wife. Instead, he expresses a different concept: that the wife can and should find in her relationship with Christ—who is the one Lord of both the spouses—the motivation of that relationship with her husband which flows from the very essence of marriage and of the family. Such a relationship, however, is not one of one-sided domination. . . . The husband and the wife are in fact "subject to one another," and are mutually subordinated to one another. . . .

Love excludes every kind of subjection whereby the wife might become a servant or a slave of the husband, an object of unilateral domination. Love makes the husband simultaneously subject to the wife, and thereby subject to the Lord himself, just as the wife to the husband. The community or unity which they should establish through marriage is constituted by a reciprocal donation of self, which is also a mutual subjection. Christ is the source and at the same time the model of that subjection, which, being reciprocal "out of reverence for Christ," confers on the conjugal union a profound and mature character.

In the Letter to the Ephesians we are, I would say, witnesses of a particular meeting of that mystery with the essence of the vocation to marriage.

—Blessed John Paul II, *Theology of the Body* Audience, August 11, 1982

Grow!

1. Do you find it more challenging to "die to self" in big ways (such as relocating for your spouse's promotion even if you don't want to move) or in small ways (your spouse likes the dishwasher to be loaded in a certain way)? How often do you insist on your own way? How can you be more sensitive to the needs and desires of one another? *(Those around you).*

_____

_____

_____

_____

_____

_____

2. Do you trust that your spouse loves you unconditionally and wants the best for you? What things can you do to insure that your spouse can trust you in this way? Do you give your husband or wife a reason to trust you? To distrust you? Discuss with one another.

_____

_____

_____

_____

_____

_____

3. What fears might you harbor about the roles for men and women that St. Paul describes? Men, as the "head of the wife" (Ephesians 5:23), do you fear becoming overbearing or selfish? Women, as being "subject to your husbands" (5:21), do you fear being manipulated or taken advantage of? What attitudes could you each adopt that would prevent this from happening?

_____

_____

_____

_____

_____

_____

4. In a society of gender confusion, how do you demonstrate a clearer image of masculinity and femininity? Do you let your husband "be the man" or your wife "be the woman," and what exactly does that mean to you?

_____

_____

_____

_____

_____

5. How can you, as a couple, grow more in unity? How can the sacraments help you to do so? How about the example of other Christian married couples in your parish or community?

_____

_____

_____

_____

_____

_____

▶ In the Spotlight
Love Is Total Surrender

Priests undergo long years of preparation in seminaries. So do all religious, male and female. But who gets preparation for marriage, and where is its novitiate? Frankly, it should begin at the father's or mother's knee . . . by seeing the parents' example. . . . The boy and girl about to marry are "in love." But do they love? Do they understand that theirs is the vocation to love—and to love so well that their children will learn love by just being their children and going into the school of their love? Do they comprehend that love is total surrender? Do they comprehend that it is the surrender to one another, for the love of God and each other? Do they understand that love never uses the pronoun "I" and is neither selfish nor self-centered? On the answer to these questions depends so much. Who can truthfully say, when they are entering marriage, that they know the answers?

The two become one. The man and the woman leave parents and home and cleave to one another, becoming one flesh. This means a surrender, a giving of oneself until, in truth, two are one flesh, one mind, one heart, one soul. For those who understand this—and alas, how few they are—the veil of faith becomes gossamer thin, especially at Communion, when husband and wife become one in the heart of Christ. That is where this oneness is felt most by those who believe, and believing, see.

—Catherine de Hueck Doherty

Reflect!

1. In what ways do you "die" for your spouse? In what ways do you need to "die" more? (Remember, there are no small sacrifices in God's eyes.)

2. Reflect on the following Scripture passages. How does each one relate to the themes in Ephesians 5:21-33?

For just as the body is one and has many members, and all the members of the body, though many, are one body, so it is with Christ. For in the one Spirit we were all baptized into one body—Jews or Greeks, slaves or free—and we were all made to drink of one Spirit. (1 Corinthians 12:12-13)

Speaking the truth in love, we must grow up in every way into him who is the head, into Christ, from whom the whole body, joined and knit together by every ligament with which it is equipped, as each part is working properly, promotes the body's growth in building itself up in love. (Ephesians 4:15-16)

If then there is any encouragement in Christ, any consolation from love, any sharing in the Spirit, any compassion and sympathy, make my joy complete: be of the same mind, having the same love, being in full accord and of one mind. Do nothing from selfish ambition or conceit, but in humility regard others as better than yourselves. Let each of you look not to your own interests, but to the interests of others. Let the same mind be in you that was in Christ Jesus,
who, though he was in the form of God,
did not regard equality with God
as something to be exploited,
but emptied himself,
taking the form of a slave,
being born in human likeness.
And being found in human form,
he humbled himself
and became obedient to the point of death—
even death on a cross. (Philippians 2:1-8)

Then [Jesus] poured water into a basin and began to wash the disciples' feet and to wipe them with the towel that was tied around him. . . .

After he had washed their feet, had put on his robe, and had returned to the table, he said to them, "Do you know what I have done to you? You call me Teacher and Lord—and you are right, for that is what I am. So if I, your Lord and Teacher, have washed your feet, you also ought to wash one another's feet. For I have set you an example, that you also should do as I have done to you." (John 13:5, 12-15)

A capable wife who can find?
    She is far more precious than jewels.
The heart of her husband trusts in her,
    and he will have no lack of gain.
She does him good, and not harm,
    all the days of her life. . . .
Strength and dignity are her clothing,
    and she laughs at the time to come.
She opens her mouth with wisdom,
    and the teaching of kindness is on her tongue.
She looks well to the ways of her household,
    and does not eat the bread of idleness.
Her children rise up and call her happy;
    her husband too, and he praises her:
"Many women have done excellently,
    but you surpass them all."
Charm is deceitful, and beauty is vain,
    but a woman who fears the LORD is to be praised.
(Proverbs 31:10-12, 25-30)

Becoming One by Submitting to Christ

Madison Avenue likes to emphasize the "me" mentality and looking out for "number one." Yet we have found a wellspring of joy and love through the direction of Ephesians 5, which calls us to do exactly the opposite. We are called to "die to self" to help our spouse. There are little ways we can die to self: losing sleep to take care of a child while the other rests, ironing your spouse's shirt instead of watching a show, taking extra time to plan a date night, or rubbing your spouse's feet when all you really want to do is to read. We have found that our love grows when we take these steps. However, it's not just in laying down our lives for each other that we truly become one. It also happens when together we lay our lives before Christ, no matter how difficult the situation.

After twelve years of marriage, we encountered a crisis that we could never have imagined. It was a nightmare, and the circumstances were out of our control. We had to trust in God completely and recommit ourselves to him every day. We submitted this cross to Christ, knowing that we don't get to choose the crosses we bear; he never promised us that. We decided to believe that somehow things would get better and to submit to whatever outcome God chose. We clung to the truth that eventually, the light would overcome the darkness.

During this time of complete submission to Christ, we discovered that we were expecting our fourth child. Feeling overwhelmed and stressed out, we thought it was bad timing. Well, we were wrong. This pregnancy helped us to focus on what was most important in our lives: family, love, and submitting ourselves completely to Christ through one another. We embraced this pregnancy with abundant joy and couldn't have asked for a greater gift in our time of despair. Our baby was born before all the turmoil ended, and she is the most wonderful symbol of

God's love that he could have ever given us. Our marriage and family life were strengthened because of this beautiful gift. We decided to name her Hope, because throughout all of our anxiety and worry, we had to place our hope in Christ daily. The deep love we shared as a couple, along with God, created this baby at a most dire time. Our love for each other grew stronger than ever.

Since then our family has grown to five children! We keep our marriage first by sharing a weekly holy hour, attending daily Mass as often as possible, and having regular date nights. We know that when we submit our marriage to Christ and put him first, all else falls into place. He always knows best. Sometimes we just need to be reminded of that truth.

—Lisa and Phil, Atchison, Kansas

Act!

1. Identify any areas that the devil can exploit or use to breed mistrust between you and your spouse. For example, does your spouse have full access to your e-mails, social-networking IDs, text messages, PINs, and passwords? If not, why not? Open up every part of your life to your spouse, and ask that your spouse open every part of their life to you.

2. Is there one thing that you really wish your spouse would try or do—something that brings you joy? Decide to take turns "sacrificing" for one another. Each spouse can choose whatever they would like to do with the other. For example, take turns planning a date. Let your spouse be in charge of every detail, and allow yourself to be led, going along with whatever they choose. Or allow your spouse to plan an activity that they enjoy even if you don't, such as playing golf or going for a long walk.

▶ In the Spotlight
Drawing on the Grace of the Sacrament of Marriage

We met at our local Catholic Church. I [Sean] was a youth minister and she [Erin] was a youth ministry volunteer. On our first date, we went to a meeting of a young-adult prayer group. What a great start! We had both been raised by good parents who had led us to a fairly strong experience of our Catholic faith, but like so many kids, we had drifted from that faith through the high school and college years. Now we were back and going through what we referred to as our "conversion": on fire for our faith and doing our best to live it out with daily Mass, frequent confession, and lots of Rosaries. After a year of dating, which included mostly church activities and prayer, we were engaged. A year later we were married, with a great foundation laid under us.

The Lord blessed us with three children in the first six years of marriage, followed by a six-year break and then a fourth child. So fifteen years and four kids later, we are still together . . . but only by the grace of God—literally.

You see, unfortunately, our marriage quickly became all too average and typical. The business of life with a growing family, the stress of just trying to make ends meet, and a lack of real effort to give our marriage what it needed to thrive left the relationship pretty empty. We went through the ups and downs that most couples do, but after a while, the downs seemed to outweigh the ups. Occasionally my wife became so frustrated that in the middle of a heated argument, she would even throw out the "D" word.

And that's when we would be truly tested to die to ourselves.

In fact, there was nothing specifically horrible that either of us had done—no lying, cheating, stealing, addiction, or abuse.

page 74 | Session 4

But just like the analogy of the frog that will sit in a pot of water while it heats to boiling and never jump out, we had just about let our marriage die by the slow simmer of neglect. So what saved it? Our personal commitment to the sacrament that we are.

More than just keeping our promise to an oath, we believe in our heart of hearts and the depth of our souls that we *are* a sacrament. And we know that this sacrament is something much bigger than either one of us—certainly much bigger than our own selfish desire to follow the temptation that leads to giving up on "this crummy marriage" and jumping the fence of divorce to see if the grass is really greener on the other side.

And if I can point to one single source that enables us to maintain our commitment to the sacrament, it is the sacrament itself. I guess that makes it a chicken-or-egg kind of thing that I will leave to those wiser than me to figure out. But what I believe is that because we honor our sacrament for what it truly is, God honors our faithfulness with the grace we need to stay committed to it.

And now that we *are* working on our marriage, learning to give it the time and attention it needs, things are certainly getting better. Yes, we made plenty of mistakes and waited way too long to get to this point, but . . . we're still here, still together. And that's what makes all the dying to self so life-giving.

—Sean and Erin, Scottsdale, Arizona

Unleashing the Virtues

Colossians 3:12-17

¹²As God's chosen ones, holy and beloved, clothe yourselves with compassion, kindness, humility, meekness, and patience. ¹³Bear with one another and, if anyone has a complaint against another, forgive each other; just as the Lord has forgiven you, so you also must forgive. ¹⁴Above all, clothe yourselves with love, which binds everything together in perfect harmony.

> The state of marriage is one that requires more virtue and constancy than any other. It is a perpetual exercise in mortification.
> —St. Francis de Sales

¹⁵And let the peace of Christ rule in your hearts, to which indeed you were called in the one body. And be thankful. ¹⁶Let the word of Christ dwell in you richly; teach and admonish one another in all wisdom; and with gratitude in your hearts sing psalms, hymns, and spiritual songs to God. ¹⁷And whatever you do, in word or deed, do everything in the name of the Lord Jesus, giving thanks to God the Father through him.

St. Paul's Letter to the Colossians is theologically deep but also very practical. It unpacks what the Christian life (and marriage) looks like on a daily basis—when the rubber meets the road, so to speak. St. Paul was fighting growing heresies that were erupting within the church in Colossae. He sought throughout the letter, and specifically in this passage, to calm growing tensions by reminding the community that Christ is bigger than the personal issues, agendas, pride, or ignorance of its members. We see Christ constantly in word, in sacrament, and in one another! God's presence, in Christ, is right before us, veiled and unveiled, if only we have the eyes to see (Matthew 13:16; Luke 10:23-24).

This passage is speaking to the natural human tension that is unleashed when we try to live what we proclaim to believe. We fail. We fall. And still, God is with us, calling us to do better, to be more—to "be perfect" (Matthew 5:48). St. Paul is challenging the burgeoning church in Colossae —and us, as well—to think differently, to "set [our] minds on things that are above, not on things that are on earth" (Colossians 3:2) and to "put on Christ" (Galatians 3:27, KJV).

St. Paul's Letter to the Colossians is divided into doctrine (what we believe) and practice (how we live it out). We face the same "divide" in marriage. It's easy to say, "I love you," but it's the living it out—"daily" (Luke 9:23)—that is difficult. When it comes to the Sacrament of Matrimony and how we approach it, we must think in heavenly, not earthly, ways, as St. Paul reminds us (Colossians 3:1-3) just prior to this passage.

Take a moment and pray through these six verses from Colossians again. Within these 135 words is the pearl of great price that countless married couples seek but rarely find. This passage contains within it the golden ticket, the secret to a happy and harmonious marriage.

The command to "clothe yourselves with compassion, kindness, humility, meekness, and patience" (Colossians 3:12) is an active one. These virtues do not happen by mere osmosis. There must be an intentionality on our part, a willingness to be led by the Spirit, to be humble before God and others, and to seek virtue as a response to the grace God has poured into our hearts as his "chosen ones" (3:12).

When St. Paul implores us to "forgive each other" (Colossians 3:13), he's not encouraging forgiveness as a benevolent and noble gesture. In this command (it's not a suggestion), he is echoing Christ's words given to us in the Lord's Prayer (Matthew 6:14-15) and unearthing a nugget of sublime wisdom—namely, that we are most like God when we forgive. Yes, to err is human, but to forgive—that is indeed divine (Luke 23:34).

In this treatise on the call to daily virtue, it is fitting that we would be called to focus specifically on love, which is the unending virtue that "binds everything together in perfect harmony" (Colossians 3:14). Assuredly, when the love between a husband and wife is authentic, selfless, and pure, the home is a happy one regardless of any finite stresses—financial, health, or otherwise—that the family is experiencing.

> We are most like God when we forgive.

In studying this passage, we can look to the saints to show us how to live it out. St. Joseph was given the mission of protecting and providing for the Holy Family, which had been placed in peril by a homicidal king. He was consistently invited to "let the peace of Christ rule" in his heart (Colossians 3:15). Our Blessed Mother, Mary, had "the word of Christ dwell" in her richly (3:16), eliciting in her the Magnificat, her song of praise and thankfulness (Luke 1:46-55). In the Holy Family, we find intercessory allies for every married couple and models of true virtue, embodying a posture of constant gratitude to the Lord regardless of circumstances or sufferings. They are also a constant reminder of how we ought to treat one another "in word or deed," all the while "giving thanks to God the Father through" Jesus (Colossians 3:17). That disposition of constant gratitude to God alleviates many of the daily stresses, defuses the senseless arguments, and avoids a myriad of potential sins by unlocking the grace of the virtues.

Disagreements are a natural part of marriage. Fighting, too, is natural. The word "intimacy" comes from a Latin term that literally means "to make the innermost known." With this in mind, it should not shock us that when a couple becomes more intimate—not just with their bodies but with their very souls—some difficult discussions and spiritual attacks will occur. The devil hates marriage, as evidenced by his incessant attacks upon it. If, then, a couple truly seek to have a holy and godly marriage, they should expect to see evil at work around them (1 Peter 5:8; Romans 7:21).

Many arguments between a husband and wife could be easily avoided if the conversation preceding it involved greater humility and different questions. This is the virtue and approach to which St. Paul is calling all of us—then and now—when we are joined and bound together in Christ Jesus. A holy life is a virtuous life. A holy and healthy marriage, too, necessitates that a husband and wife both be striving for lives of heroic virtue. Their love embodies and enlivens faith and hope and, most certainly, love in and for God and one another (Colossians 3:14).

By living a virtuous life in a world that often does not understand or believe in true love, sacrificial marriage, or deeper intimacy, you (as a couple) become a living, breathing "apologetic," a way of teaching the faith. You draw all you encounter to a tangible encounter with Christ within the sacrament that God himself created.

Understand!

1. What should St. Paul's challenge remind the Colossian church (and us) about the power of grace and what their relationship to Christ affords them more than others?

_____

_____

_____

_____

_____

_____

2. Why is forgiveness emphasized so primarily here? Why do you think St. Paul points to forgiveness as such a key component in living out this call to virtue? How is forgiving different from "putting up with something" or "forgetting about something?"

_____

_____

_____

_____

_____

_____

3. Why is love the greatest virtue? Explain why in as tangible terms as you can. Give practical examples of what love is and is not in your opinion. Now, give tangible examples of what St. Paul says love is, using this passage, as well as 1 Corinthians 13:1-13 and Romans 12:9-18.

_____

_____

_____

_____

_____

_____

4. St. Paul admonishes us that peace must rule in our hearts (Colossians 3:15). What kind of peace do you think he was talking about? What can couples do to usher in peace and unleash it amid the daily turmoil? What is one thing you could do as a couple to make this even more of a reality?

_____

_____

_____

_____

_____

5. What do you think St. Paul means when he advises the community to "do everything in the name of the Lord Jesus" (Colossians 3:17)? What does this look like in daily life? What do our words and our deeds say about us?

_____

_____

_____

_____

_____

_____

▶ In the Spotlight
The *Catechism of the Catholic Church* on Virtue

Human virtues acquired by education, by deliberate acts and by a perseverance ever-renewed in repeated efforts are purified and elevated by divine grace. With God's help, they forge character and give facility in the practice of the good. The virtuous man is happy to practice them. (1810)

It is not easy for man, wounded by sin, to maintain moral balance. Christ's gift of salvation offers us the grace necessary to persevere in the pursuit of the virtues. Everyone should always ask for this grace of light and strength, frequent the sacraments, cooperate with the Holy Spirit, and follow his calls to love what is good and shun evil. (1811)

The practice of all the virtues is animated and inspired by charity, which "binds everything together in perfect harmony" (Colossians 3:14); it is the *form of the virtues*; it articulates and orders them among themselves; it is the source and the goal of their

Christian practice. Charity upholds and purifies our human
ability to love, and raises it to the supernatural perfection of
divine love. (1827)

Grow!

1. The word of God is supposed to dwell in us richly (Colossians
   3:16). What do you do to allow the Word of God (the person of
   Jesus Christ) dwell in you *richly*? Be specific. In what ways as well
   do you actively seek to allow the word of God (Sacred Scripture) to
   take root in your soul and daily life? What is one thing you could
   do as a couple to make this even more of a reality?

   _____

   _____

   _____

   _____

   _____

   _____

2. How do you show your love and your respect to your spouse *daily*?
   Give three examples.

   _____

   _____

   _____

   _____

   _____

3. How gentle do you think you are with your spouse? How com-
   passionate? How patient? What does your spouse think? Is there

a big difference in your perceptions? Ask your spouse to show you specific ways that you could grow in these virtues.

_____

_____

_____

_____

_____

_____

4. How do you show your appreciation for your spouse? How do you affirm him or her? Take a couple of minutes and find five things to affirm about your spouse. Take turns offering those affirmations to one another. How could you regularly practice gratitude to each other?

_____

_____

_____

_____

_____

_____

5. Christians are God's living, breathing "billboards" on earth. Our words and deeds do or do not point back to him. So how does your marriage glorify God? Give tangible examples. What are some additional ways you could give glory to God through your marriage?

_____

_____

_____

_____

_____

_____

▶ In the Spotlight
Love Is Proved by Deeds

The love . . . of which we are speaking is not that based on the passing lust of the moment nor does it consist in pleasing words only, but in the deep attachment of the heart which is expressed in action, since love is proved by deeds. This outward expression of love in the home demands not only mutual help but must go further; must have as its primary purpose that man and wife help each other day by day in forming and perfecting themselves in the interior life, so that through their partnership in life they may advance ever more and more in virtue, and above all that they may grow in true love toward God and their neighbor. . . . For all men of every condition, in whatever honorable walk of life they may be, can and ought to imitate that most perfect example of holiness placed before man by God, namely Christ Our Lord, and by God's grace to arrive at the summit of perfection, as is proved by the example set us of many saints.

—Pope Pius XI, *Caste Connubii*, 23

All the Christian virtues should flourish in the family, unity should thrive, and the example of its virtuous living should shine brightly. . . . The Christian family is a sacred institution. If it totters, if the norms which the divine Redeemer laid down for it are rejected or ignored, then the very foundation of the state tremble; civil society stands betrayed and in peril. Everyone suffers.

—Blessed John XXIII, *Ad Petri Cathedram*, 57, 58

Reflect!

1. Would your friends and co-workers describe you as virtuous? Does your life point others toward God or toward self?

2. Reflect on the following Scripture passages about growing in virtue:

You must make every effort to support your faith with goodness, and goodness with knowledge, and knowledge with self-control, and self-control with endurance, and endurance with godliness, and godliness with mutual affection, and mutual affection with love. For if these things are yours and are increasing among you, they keep you from being ineffective and unfruitful in the knowledge of our Lord Jesus Christ. For anyone who lacks these things is short-sighted and blind, and is forgetful of the cleansing of past sins. (2 Peter 1:5-9)

Let your adornment be the inner self with the lasting beauty of a gentle and quiet spirit, which is very precious in God's sight. (1 Peter 3:4)

You are witnesses, and God also, how pure, upright, and blameless our conduct was toward you believers. As you know, we dealt with each one of you like a father with his children, urging and encouraging you and pleading that you lead a life worthy of God, who calls you into his own kingdom and glory. (1 Thessalonians 2:10-12)

Rash words are like sword thrusts, / but the tongue of the wise brings healing. (Proverbs 12:18)

Then Peter came and said to him, "Lord, if another member of the church sins against me, how often should I forgive? As many as seven times?" Jesus said to him, "Not seven times, but, I tell you, seventy-seven times." (Matthew 18:21-22)

▶ In the Spotlight
The Virtue of Waiting on the Other

We had been married eight years and were living the life we'd dreamed of. We lived in our hometown near family and gathered several times a week to share life together. Our best friends were a part of our daily lives. We had a vibrant home parish where the Spirit was fully alive. We had a lovely house that we'd spent much time, money, and sweat making our home. It was the perfect place to raise our growing young family. Or so we thought.

While we had both separately felt the Lord starting to stir within us and our marriage, neither of us knew what it was. As time would reveal, the Lord would call us away from the comfort, security, and love of all that we had around us. He gently but very firmly invited us to move to North Georgia with another young family to serve in running Life Teen Camp Covecrest and building a Catholic community. It was so far removed from anything we'd known or done.

The unknown was, depending upon which of us you had asked, incredibly frightening or incredibly exhilarating. Jason has always been more adventurous, and this new opportunity the Lord had presented stirred in him very "wild at heart" emotions. He was ready to pack the truck. I [Melissa] have always been a home-and-family kind of girl. I did not see these new possibilities as an opportunity but as a frightening upheaval of all that I loved. As you can imagine, these differing inclinations were fertile ground for tension in a relatively young marriage. It was a time of intense prayer and discernment for us, who, as a couple, were new to discerning together something so life changing.

In the midst of it, Jason went on his annual men's mission trip. These trips had always been fruitful for our marriage and family. Jason would return home renewed, focused, and determined to live more boldly for the kingdom. That year, while Jason was gone, I filled pages and pages of my journal with fears and anxieties, not only of what the Lord might be calling us as a couple to do, but also what Jason might say about it all when he came home reinvigorated.

There was a strange tension in the reunion. I was on eggshells waiting for Jason to say the words "I know you're not ready, but we need to go." Those dreaded words never came, and finally, tearfully, I shared my fears of what might be spoken. Jason listened and then tenderly and compassionately said, "*I* am not going to make this decision for us. *We* are going to make this decision for us. Nothing is going to happen until you have peace about it. I will wait for you for as long as it takes." To hear Jason put his desires and excitement aside selflessly for me gave me a true freedom to hear the Lord myself.

The discernment continued, and I wrestled with God in many rounds. Jason gently and patiently waited and fervently prayed for his bride to hear the Lord's voice. Finally, on the ninth day of a novena to the Holy Spirit, the wrestling ended, and God claimed a gentle but joyous victory. I knew Jason's gentle and patient love, and it firmly planted a deep trust and unity in our marriage.

—Jason and Melissa, Tiger, Georgia

Act!

1. How do we clothe ourselves in love? Take time to think of and identify one small random act of kindness you can do each day for your spouse . . . and then do it.

2. Pay attention to verbal tone and body language. Give your spouse the right to call you out or walk away if your tone is anything less than positive or gentle.

▶ In the Spotlight
The Need for Conversion

It takes conversion to be able to love another; it takes deep conversion to love that person deeply. If husbands and wives understood this and put it into practice, divorces would vanish. And so would domestic fights and bickering and pouting and shouting disappear. Sympathetic listening to each other in differences of opinion would blossom. Each spouse would desire to do what the other prefers in practical matters. When one slips through half advertence or momentary weakness, loving forgiveness would bring immediate healing. The children would see and experience what genuine family life looks like. Even though it may be a gradual and even slow process, they, too, would begin to practice what they see.

—Fr. Thomas Dubay, SM, *Deep Conversion, Deep Prayer*

An Invitation to Intimacy

Revelation 19:1, 6-16

¹After this I heard what seemed to be the loud voice of a great multitude in heaven, saying,

"Hallelujah!

Salvation and glory and power to our God." . . .

⁶Then I heard what seemed to be the voice of a great multitude, like the sound of many waters and like the sound of mighty thunderpeals, crying out,

"Hallelujah!

For the Lord our God
    the Almighty reigns.

⁷Let us rejoice and exult
    and give him the glory,

for the marriage of the Lamb has come,
    and his bride has made herself ready;

⁸to her it has been granted to be clothed
    with fine linen, bright and pure"—

for the fine linen is the righteous deeds of the saints.

⁹And the angel said to me, "Write this: Blessed are those who are invited to the marriage supper of the Lamb." And he said to me, "These are true words of God." ¹⁰Then I fell down at his feet to worship him, but he said to me, "You must not do that! I am a fellow servant with you and your comrades who hold the testimony of Jesus. Worship God! For the testimony of Jesus is the spirit of prophecy."

> This human communion [marriage] . . . is deepened by lives of the common faith and by the Eucharist received together.
> —*Catechism of the Catholic Church*, 1644

¹¹Then I saw heaven opened, and there was a white horse! Its rider is called Faithful and True, and in righteousness he judges and makes war. ¹²His eyes are like a flame of fire, and on his head are many diadems; and he has a name inscribed that no one knows but himself.

¹³He is clothed in a robe dipped in blood, and his name is called The Word of God. ¹⁴And the armies of heaven, wearing fine linen, white and pure, were following him on white horses. ¹⁵From his mouth comes a sharp sword with which to strike down the nations, and he will rule them with a rod of iron; he will tread the wine press of the fury of the wrath of God the Almighty. ¹⁶On his robe and on his thigh he has a name inscribed, "King of kings and Lord of lords."

Like marriage, the Book of Revelation is often misunderstood. Some have interpreted it as an end-of-the-world scenario, which can invoke fear and lead people to see the book as a set of secrets to be deciphered and unlocked in order to foresee the future. There's nothing to fear, however, because Revelation is not intended to scare us. Revelation is a book of hope. The main "theme" of Revelation is that of a wedding. Remember what we said in the first session—that God himself is the creator and author of marriage? Well, the Holy Spirit, who is Wisdom, wanted to be sure that we didn't miss that point before the inspired Scriptures were completed in Revelation. The ancient title for Revelation is *Apokalypsis*, which literally means, "pull back the veil." That is wedding imagery.

Marriage is used as a symbolic element throughout Scripture to describe God's relationship with his people (Isaiah 54:5, 62:4; Jeremiah 31:32; Hosea 2:16-20; Ezekiel 16:8, 2 Samuel 17:3, Malachi 2:14-15). The final chapters of Revelation depict a wedding liturgy, which this passage is explicitly "unveiling." The Church—all of us who are baptized—are Christ's bride (2 Corinthians 11:2). This matrimonial allusion is an analogy of proportionality, as St. Thomas Aquinas might say, helping us to understand a bit about the love of God, though we can never really understand his great love fully.

The metaphor of the Church as the bride and Christ as the bridegroom is foundational to our understanding of Christ's intimate and eternal presence with us. If it reflects the reality, as Scripture affirms in passages like the ones above and in many others (see Ephesians 5:21-33; Matthew 22:1-14), then we can understand the Mass as a wedding liturgy (and fittingly so, given the topic of this study and this book). Some of the early Church Fathers often pointed to this more "mystical" understanding of the Mass itself as a wedding in their writings and homilies. For instance, St. John Chrysostom observed: "The Church was made from the side of Christ, and he united himself to her in a spiritual intercourse. Think about all this . . . marriage is an image of the presence of Christ" (*Homily* 12).

These verses begin with a chorus of praise (Revelation 19:1) as we pray alongside the angels in adoration, proclaiming, "Hallelujah"—translated as "Praise the Lord!" (the Hebrew is *Hallĕlūyāh*; the Greek, *Allēlouia*). And this praise should resound in the heart of every Catholic, because we've been invited to a wedding—but not as a mere spectator. No, we are "blessed" (19:9) to be the bride, bestowed with a splendor that radiates God's glory.

The the Eucharist constantly points all couples back to the perfect Triune love of Father, Son, and Holy Spirit.

The entrance of the hero on the white horse (Revelation 19:11) is something straight out of a movie. It's the proverbial knight in shining armor, arriving on a noble steed, only this knight has fire in his eyes, a robe dipped in blood, and an army behind him (19:12-14). The imagery of the blood-stained robe and the wrath-filled trenching of the wine press (19:15) echoes back to a scene from Isaiah 63:1-6. The sharp sword coming forth from the mouth of Christ (19:15) recalls a scene in the Book of Wisdom where the divine word comes out of heaven like a warrior:

Your all-powerful word leapt from heaven, from the
  royal throne,
into the midst of the land that was doomed,
a stern warrior
carrying the sharp sword of your authentic command,
and stood and filled all things with death,
and touched heaven while standing on the earth.
(Wisdom 18:15-16)

The army following this heroic warrior is comprised of the saints, named and unnamed, who have gone before us in faith, clothed in righteousness (Revelation 19:8) and marked with the seal of baptism and confirmation (9:4; 19:16; CCC, 1296). The army is comprised of those who have shared in God's divine life and enjoyed the deepest intimacy with God while on earth through the sacraments. They are dressed in fine linen, since the blood of the Lamb (baptism, reconciliation) and the fruit of the vine (the Eucharist) have preserved them, not condemned them (19:13-15).

So what is the purpose of all this mystical symbolism and imagery of marriage? Why the analogy of the bride and groom? Why is this the example through which God wants to teach us about our relationship to him? God is love (1 John 4:8)—it's that simple! As perfect love, God desires to share that perfect love. Thanks to the cross and through baptism, we are invited into that love in an intimate way. Christ, the groom, has essentially proposed to the Church, his bride.

We are called into an intimate relationship, one of a pure lover, in which we can become one with God. He's a jealous God, not because he is egomaniacal, but rather, because he knows that no other love can begin to compare to his. It's a reminder that even if our own spouse lets us down, God never will. It's an invitation and a challenge too for us to live no longer for ourselves (2 Corinthians 5:15) but for Christ himself and for the person of Christ within our spouse. While we will not attain perfection on earth, we are still called to pursue it (Matthew 5:48).

So beautiful is the scene and so overwhelmed is St. John by the glory radiating around him and the revelation of this invitation into intimacy with God that he prostrates himself before an angel (Revelation 19:10). As we saw in the first verse (19:1), in this vision of heaven, we have been lifted up. We are not worshipping God in imitation of the angels but alongside the angels, which our Church proclaims is true at every single Mass. During the Catholic liturgy, we are being invited to experience a foretaste of heaven. We are shown a glimpse of the heavenly throne room, where the saints and angels are worshipping God—even though we cannot see them on earth. At every Mass, Christ is coming into our midst—crashing into our existence—to love and save us.

The Eucharist, in this way, offers us indescribable intimacy with God; at the same time, it elevates the marital intimacy between the husband and wife and the fraternal intimacy between the faithful. In the Eucharist, Christ offers himself completely—body, blood, soul, and divinity—as a sacrificial gift to his bride, the Church. This is precisely the type of self-forgetful, sacrificial love to which a husband and wife are called through the Eucharist, which deepens their covenant with both God and one another. Indeed, as Cardinal Angelo Scola pointed out in *The Nuptial Mystery*, "Acts of conjugal love in particular are called to be rooted in the Eucharist, in order to be manifestations and actualizations of Christ's love for his Church: an integral gift of self, without reserve, which always implies body and soul."

Thus, the more deeply a husband and wife comprehend the sacrificial nature of the Holy Eucharist, the more profoundly aware that couple will become of Christ's presence within their own relationship. In the conjugal expression of self-gift, husband and wife are called not to *take* but to *receive* one another; likewise, "to receive communion is to receive Christ himself who has offered himself to us" (CCC 1382).

Only when we learn to receive the Lord before us, veiled beneath the guise of common bread, will we be able as spouses to fully receive the Lord across from us, present within our husband or wife.

Our regular reception of the Eucharist offers us a profound intimacy with God, a foundation upon which couples can actually unleash the virtues and enjoy the healthy married life described throughout this Bible study. The Eucharistic sacrifice calls all couples to an ever-deepening understanding of selfless love for one another. When this happens, married love cannot grow stagnant and will leave neither spouse wanting. Revealing God's love at every turn, the Eucharist constantly points all couples back to the perfect Triune love of Father, Son, and Holy Spirit.

Understand!

1. Why would God choose to compare salvation and eternal life with him to a marriage? Why not just stick with some other analogy of potter and clay or parent and child? What does that tell us about the mind and heart of God, the creator of marriage?

_____

_____

_____

_____

_____

2. How does the wedding garment, fine and pure (Revelation 19:8), relate to us today? Where and how do we ensure that we are adorned in the proper garment, exuding holiness and readiness?

_____

_____

_____

_____

_____

_____

3. Who are the "blessed" (Revelation 19:9), and why is that important? When and how are we invited to this feast? When and how do we "RSVP"? Ponder the sacraments as you explain your answer.

_____

_____

_____

_____

_____

4. Why the white horse? Why the diadems? Why the blood-dipped robe? What is God revealing to us in these symbolic images?

_____

_____

_____

_____

_____

5. Do you believe that heaven is as it's described in this passage? Why or why not? What do you base your thoughts on? Explain.

_____

_____

_____

_____

_____

The Challenge of the Book of Revelation

The Book of Revelation is challenging because it is written in a specific type of biblical literature, namely, apocalyptic. It's not really intended to be read as a historical narrative, like the gospels, for instance. Revelation communicates through imagery and symbolism, utilizing colors, numbers, and other symbolic language to relate truths in an allegorical way. The color white, for instance, denotes purity and victory. Black denotes death, scarlet symbolizes immorality, and red points to violence and bloodshed. The number seven demonstrates completeness, while six denotes imperfection. A close reading reveals that crowns symbolize authority, horns mean power, and thunder is usually associated with the voice of God.

The apocalyptic style demands a great deal of prayer, study, and contextual analysis to truly comprehend or appreciate. Approved ancillary texts that are faithful to Church teachings serve as invaluable study aids that quickly make this book far less intimidating. Fortunately, the Catholic Church has centuries of wisdom to draw from, including that offered by its saints. The Church helps us unpack Revelation in the manner it was intended—free of fear, personal bias, or preconceived ideas—and sheds light on the beauty that exists within this most misunderstood work.

Grow!

1. Do you trust your spouse enough to ask him or her what your weaknesses are? Do you look to and expect your spouse to help you in overcoming bad habits or patterns of sin? Do you ask your

spouse to regularly pray for you? How often do you pray for your husband or wife?

_____

_____

_____

_____

_____

_____

2. Do you and your spouse usually attend Mass together? Do you see yourselves as encountering Christ as a couple? How might praying together in adoration help your marriage?

_____

_____

_____

_____

_____

3. How can a regular practice of examining your conscience and going to confession help you grow closer to God *and* your spouse? How often do you ask God to show you ways in which you could love your spouse better?

_____

_____

_____

_____

_____

_____

4. What are your priorities in life? Do you each put God first? If so, how do you demonstrate that, practically speaking? What would be some additional ways you could demonstrate it?

_____

_____

_____

_____

_____

_____

5. Is your spouse second in your life only to God? Again, in what ways do you demonstrate that right order? If not, why not? Have children superseded your spouse as the priority? Has "occupation" replaced "vocation" in the battle for your energy and focus?

_____

_____

_____

_____

_____

▶ In the Spotlight
The Perfect Union

As joyful as an earthly marriage might be, death threatens its duration. Even before death, the sin of the spouses can cast doubt upon their union. No marriage is perfect. We see this in the Church's wedding rite: As soon as the spouses have exchanged their vows, the priest prays, "May the Lord in his goodness strengthen your consent." It is as if the Church is asking God to make up for the weakness in the vows, a weakness that will always be there because of original sin.

Recall that the first manifestation of original sin in Adam and Eve is that they realized they were naked and clothed themselves. They did this before the Lord came back into the garden. This means that they were ashamed even in front of each other. There were aspects of themselves that they held back and hid from one another. Their unity was compromised.

The wedding of the New Jerusalem with the Lamb is total. It has none of this weakness or uncertainty and will never be threatened by sin or death, for "death shall be no more" (Revelation 21:4). This is the perfect union to which holy and yet imperfect earthly marriages point.

—Fr. Richard Veras, *Wisdom for Everyday Life from the Book of Revelation*

Reflect!

1. How do you receive Communion? Do you receive the Body of Christ as a gift to your soul? Is your reception of the Eucharist rooted in a desire to grow in holiness, or do you sometimes view it as a means to an end of the liturgy?

2. Reflect on the following Scripture passages that use wedding imagery to describe God's relationship with us.

> The nations shall see your vindication,
>   and all the kings your glory;
> and you shall be called by a new name
>   that the mouth of the LORD will give.
> You shall be a crown of beauty in the hand of the LORD,
>   and a royal diadem in the hand of your God.
> You shall no more be termed Forsaken,
>   and your land shall no more be termed Desolate;

but you shall be called My Delight Is in Her,
    and your land Married;
for the LORD delights in you,
    and your land shall be married.
For as a young man marries a young woman,
    so shall your builder marry you,
and as the bridegroom rejoices over the bride,
    so shall your God rejoice over you.
(Isaiah 62:2-5)

I will greatly rejoice in the LORD,
    my whole being shall exult in my God;
for he has clothed me with the garments of salvation,
    he has covered me with the robe of righteousness,
as a bridegroom decks himself with a garland,
    and as a bride adorns herself with her jewels.
For as the earth brings forth its shoots,
    and as a garden causes what is sown in it to spring up,
so the Lord GOD will cause righteousness and praise
    to spring up before all the nations.
(Isaiah 61:10-11)

My beloved speaks and says to me:
"Arise, my love, my fair one,
    and come away;
for now the winter is past,
    the rain is over and gone.
The flowers appear on the earth;
    the time of singing has come,
and the voice of the turtle dove
    is heard in our land.
The fig tree puts forth its figs,
    and the vines are in blossom;

they give forth fragrance.
Arise, my love, my fair one,
  and come away."
(Song of Songs 2:10-13)

They came to John and said to him, "Rabbi, the one who was with you across the Jordan, to whom you testified, here he is baptizing, and all are going to him." John answered, "No one can receive anything except what has been given from heaven. You yourselves are my witnesses that I said, 'I am not the Messiah, but I have been sent ahead of him.' He who has the bride is the bridegroom. The friend of the bridegroom, who stands and hears him, rejoices greatly at the bridegroom's voice. For this reason my joy has been fulfilled. He must increase, but I must decrease." (John 3:26-30)

Then the disciples of John came to [Jesus], saying, "Why do we and the Pharisees fast often, but your disciples do not fast?" And Jesus said to them, "The wedding guests cannot mourn as long as the bridegroom is with them, can they? The days will come when the bridegroom is taken away from them, and then they will fast." (Matthew 9:14-15)

▶ In the Spotlight
Christ Expands Our Love

Mike: I come from a broken home; she comes from a strong Catholic Christian home. My home was filled with chaos; hers was filled with love and many children. Though her childhood wasn't perfect, her parents were faithful, loving, and together.

I wasn't Catholic when we got married, but my wife's reverence for the Eucharist made me yearn for it. It took seven years for me to get up the courage to join the Church, but when our marriage became sacramental, something changed. Jesus was already a growing part of our relationship, but now he was *really* there, every day. Both of us are profoundly changed each time we receive the Eucharist. It is Jesus who unites us in the covenant relationship that we share. He is what unites us in the communal banquet of his Body and Blood. His love is our bedrock. It is what we share most intimately.

As we grow older and our bodies begin to fail, and as our children grow older and leave home and we are faced with the reality of living the rest of our lives in this way, the common ground that bonds us together remains: Jesus is still there, every day.

Kate: Mike and I often talk about what it means to truly love. We believe that true love means that you want to get the other person to heaven, to be with them for all eternity. This is an amazing part of our marriage. As we fight, prod, and encourage each other, it is always in the back of my mind: "Am I helping him get to heaven, or is this about our earthly wants?"

The closest thing we have to heaven on earth is the Mass and the Eucharist. So participating in the Eucharist is paramount to our true love. Each time we take the living Christ into our bodies, we are filled with his love. Our human love is expanded with the love of Christ. To share that love (the three of us: God, Mike, and I) amplifies our true love.

On the day of our wedding, our best man made this toast: "Keep it interesting!" Throughout our life, from newlyweds, to parents, to business partners, to coaches, to Church ministers, and now as grandparents, our marriage has definitely been a journey, a journey towards heaven. Some of our journey has been rocky, but with God as our guide, it has definitely been "interesting"!

—Mike and Kate, Houston, Texas

Act!

1. Does your spouse have "carte blanche" to call you out on things that are keeping you from sainthood? Have your spouse point out three things that are acting as obstacles to your growth in holiness.

2. Go above and beyond in some way in your faith walk, individually and as a couple. Perhaps each of you could get a spiritual director. Maybe you could go on a retreat together or join a bible study. Or sign up for a weekly holy hour together.

▶ In the Spotlight
Together with the Eucharist

Take a minute and think of all the places you have met with your spouse over the past few years. Was it at work, a store, a coffeehouse, the airport, or, if you have children, on the sidelines of your school's sports fields? As a married couple for twenty-four years now, we can name plenty of places where we have met.

But there is one spot where we meet frequently and where our marriage has been showered with unbelievable graces. That spot is the Eucharist. We often attend daily Mass together or spend time in front of the Blessed Sacrament as a couple. You see, as a Catholic couple, it is in the Eucharist that we meet the One who is the source of our marriage. Whatever we are facing as a family or in our relationship, being with each other and with Jesus fully present in the Eucharist helps keep us focused on him. Young people often ask us how we have been married so long, and we are quick to reply that it isn't always easy, but we regularly pray together, especially by attending Mass and spending holy hours in Eucharistic adoration.

It wasn't always this way for us. When we were first married, we went to Mass only on Sundays and holy days of obligation. Friends began to challenge us individually to start going to Mass during the week at our parish. We were sporadic at first, and then it became like a "mini-date" for us to go to Mass together in the morning. Not only did it soon become something we wanted to do, but we quickly realized that our marriage needed it.

Then, a few years ago, a new priest arrived at our parish and started perpetual adoration. He didn't know if anyone would sign up, but was simply being obedient to what he felt God was asking him to do. We each signed up to help by taking a holy hour each week. Most of our time before the Blessed Sacrament is spent praying for our marriage, our kids (we have eight amazing children), and for any intentions that have been given to us to pray for.

Even if you as a couple can go to Mass only once during the week, you will see amazing graces in your relationship with your spouse. And spending time in front of the Blessed Sacrament as a couple can be one of the most rewarding and intimate times you can have. We believe that couples that frequently meet at the Eucharist will be couples whose marriages not only survive but blossom and thrive.

—Randy and Monica, Marietta, Georgia

Practical Pointers for Bible Study Sessions

Bible study offers us the opportunity to grow not only in our love for God's word but also in our love for one another. We don't have to be trained Scripture scholars to benefit from discussing and studying the Bible together. Bible study groups provide environments in which we can worship and pray together and strengthen our relationships with other Christians, and this is also true of married couples who want to study the Bible together. The following guidelines can help you and your spouse get started.

Getting Started

- Decide on a regular time and place to meet. Meeting on a regular basis allows you to maintain continuity without losing momentum from the previous discussion.

- Set a time limit for each session. An hour and a half is a reasonable length of time in which to have a rewarding discussion on the material contained in each of the sessions in this guide. However, you may find that a longer time is even more advantageous. If it is necessary to limit the meeting to an hour, select sections of the material that are of greatest interest to you.

- If possible, provide a separate copy of the study for each of you so that you will each have it readily available to read prior to your sessions together. Each session's Scripture text and related passages for reflection are printed in full in the guides, but you will find that a Bible is helpful for looking up other passages and cross-references. The translation provided in this guide is the New Revised Standard Version (Catholic Edition). You may also want to refer to other translations—for example, the New American Bible or the New Jerusalem Bible—to gain additional insights into the text.

Session Dynamics

- Read the material for each session in advance, and take time to consider the questions and your answers to them individually. The single most important key to any successful Bible study is being prepared in advance to discuss the material.

- Open the sessions with prayer. The prayer could be a spontaneous one, a traditional prayer such as the Our Father, or one that relates to the topic of that particular meeting. You might also want to begin some of the meetings with a song or hymn. Whatever you choose, ask the Holy Spirit to guide your discussion and study of the Scripture text presented in that session.

- Try to stick to the topic so that you won't divert the discussion from its purpose. And resist the temptation to monopolize the conversation so that each of you has an opportunity to learn from the other and about the other.

- Listen attentively to your spouse. Show respect for your spouse and his or her contributions. Encourage, support, and affirm what your spouse shares. Remember that many questions have more than one answer, and be open to a different viewpoint.

- If you disagree, do so gently and respectfully, in a way that shows that you value your spouse, and then explain your own point of view. For example, rather than saying, "You're wrong!" or "That's ridiculous!" try something like "I think I see what you're getting at, but this is how I think about it." Be careful to avoid sounding aggressive or argumentative. Who knows? You may come away with a new and deeper perspective.

- Don't be afraid of pauses and reflective moments of silence during the session. Your spouse may need some time to think about a question before putting his or her thoughts into words.

- Safeguard the privacy and dignity of your spouse by not repeating what has been shared to anyone else. That way, both you and your spouse will feel completely free to share on a deep personal level.

- End the session with prayer. Thank God for what you have learned through the discussion, and ask the Lord to help you integrate it into your life.

The Lord blesses all our efforts to come closer to him. As you spend time preparing for and meeting with your spouse, be confident in the knowledge that Christ will fill you with wisdom, insight, and grace, and the ability to see him at work in your daily life together.

Sources and Acknowledgments

Session 1: The Two Becoming One

Pope John Paul II, Apostolic Letter, *Mulieris Dignitatem*, 7, issued August 15, 1988, accessed at http://www.vatican .va/holy_father/john_paul_ii/apost_letters/documents/ hf_jp-ii_apl_15081988_mulieris-dignitatem_en.html.

Session 2: Filling the Void

Peter Kreeft, *You Can Understand the Bible* (San Francisco: Ignatius Press, 2005), 101–103.

Fulton Sheen, *Three to Get Married* (New York: Scepter Publishers, Inc., 1951), 43, 51–53.

Second Vatican Council, *Gaudium et Spes*, 48, accessed at http://www.vatican.va/archive/hist_councils/ii_vatican_council/ documents/vat-ii_cons_19651207_gaudium-et-spes_en.html.

Ronald Knox, *The Hidden Stream: Mysteries of the Christian Faith* (San Francisco: Ignatius Press, 2003), 191.

Session 3: Tearing Down False Temples

Peter Kreeft, *You Can Understand the Bible*, 239.

Peter Kreeft, *Back to Virtue* (San Francisco: Ignatius Press, 1992), 168.

Pope John Paul II, Theology of the Body Audience, October 22, 1980, 4, 5, accessed at http://www.ewtn.com/library/PAPALDOC/ jp2tb44.htm.

Session 4: On a Mission from God

Pope John Paul II, Theology of the Body Audience, August 11, 1982, accessed at http://www.ewtn.com/library/PAPALDOC/ jp2tb88.htm.

Catherine de Hueck Doherty, quoted by Teresa De Bertodano in *The Book of Catholic Wisdom* (Chicago: Loyola Press, 2001), 184.

Session 5: Your Home as the Domestic Church

Pope Pius XI, Encyclical Letter, *Casti Connubii*, 23, issued December 31, 1930, accessed at http://www.vatican.va/holy_ father/pius_xi/encyclicals/documents/hf_p-xi_enc_31121930_casti -connubii_en.html.

Pope John XXII, Encyclical l\Letter, *Ad Petri Cathedram*, 57, 58, issued June 29, 1959, accessed at http://www.vatican .va/holy_father/john_xxiii/encyclicals/documents/hf_j -xxiii_enc_29061959_ad-petri_en.html.

Thomas Dubay, SM, *Deep Conversion, Deep Prayer* (San Francisco: Ignatius Press, 2006), 71.

Session 6: The Weekly Wedding Feast

Angelo Scola, *The Nuptial Mystery* (Grand Rapids, MI: Wm. B. Eerdmans, 2005), 369–70.

Richard Veras, *Wisdom for Everyday Life from the Book of Revelation*, (Cincinnati, OH: Servant Books, 2010), 115.

Also in The Word Among Us Keys to the Bible Series

Six Sessions for Individuals or Groups

The Women of the Gospels: Missionaries of God's Love
Item# BTWFE9

Jesus' Journey to the Cross: A Love unto Death
Item# BTWGE9

Treasures Uncovered: The Parables of Jesus
Item# BTWAE5

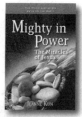

Mighty in Power: The Miracles of Jesus
Item# BTWBE6

Food from Heaven: The Eucharist in Scripture
Item# BTWCE7

Heart to Heart with God: Six Ways to Empower Your Prayer Life
Item# BTWEE8

Moved by the Spirit: God's Power at Work in His People
Item# BTWDE8

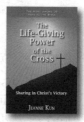

The Life-Giving Power of the Cross: Sharing in Christ's Victory
Item# BTWKE2

Money in the Kingdom of God: Six Essential Attitudes for Followers of Christ
Item# BTWHE0

Each of the Keys to the Bible study sessions features

- the full Scripture text;
- a short commentary;
- questions for reflection, discussion, and personal application;
- "In the Spotlight" sections featuring wisdom from the saints and the Church, root meanings of Greek words, fascinating historical background, and stories of faith from contemporary people.

To order call 1-800-775-9673 or order online at wau.org